THIRD EDITION

TOP NOTCH 2B

ENGLISH FOR TODAY'S WORLD

JOAN SASLOW
ALLEN ASCHER

With *Top Notch Pop* Songs and Karaoke
by Rob Morsberger

Top Notch: English for Today's World   Level 2B, Third Edition

Pearson Education, 10 Bank Street, White Plains, NY 10606 USA

Staff credits: The people who made up the *Top Notch* team are Pietro Alongi, Rhea Banker, Peter Benson, Tracey Munz Cataldo, Rosa Chapinal, Aerin Csigay, Dave Dickey, Gina DiLillo, Nancy Flaggman, Irene Frankel, Shelley Gazes, Christopher Leonowicz, Kate McLoughlin, Julie Molnar, Laurie Neaman, Sherri Pemberton, Pamela Pia, Jennifer Raspiller, Charlene Straub, Paula Van Ells, and Kenneth Volcjak.

Cover photo: Sprint/Corbis
Text composition: TSI Graphics

Library of Congress Cataloging-in-Publication Data

Saslow, Joan M.
  Top Notch : English for today's world. Fundamentals / Joan Saslow, Allen Ascher ; With Top Notch Pop Songs
  and Karaoke by Rob Morsberger. — Third Edition.
    pages cm
  Includes biographical references.
  ISBN 978-0-13-354275-2 — ISBN 978-0-13-339348-4 — ISBN 978-0-13-354277-6 — ISBN 978-0-13-354278-3   1. English language—
  Textbooks for foreign speakers. 2. English language—Problems, exercises, etc. 3. English language—Sound recordings for foreign speakers.
  I. Ascher, Allen. II. Morsberger, Robert Eustis, 1929- III. Title. IV. Title: English for today's world.
  PE1128.S2757 2015
  428.2'4--dc23

                        2013044020

Printed in the United States of America
ISBN-10: 0-13-392824-1
ISBN-13: 978-0-13-392824-2

pearsonelt.com/topnotch3e

In Memoriam

Rob Morsberger (1959–2013)

The authors wish to acknowledge their memory of and gratitude to **Rob Morsberger**, the gifted composer and songwriter of the *Top Notch Pop* Songs and Karaoke that have provided learners both language practice and pleasure.

6 2020

ABOUT THE AUTHORS

Joan Saslow

Joan Saslow has taught in a variety of programs in South America and the United States. She is author or coauthor of a number of widely used courses, some of which are *Ready to Go, Workplace Plus, Literacy Plus,* and *Summit.* She is also author of *English in Context,* a series for reading science and technology. Ms. Saslow was the series director of *True Colors* and *True Voices.* She has participated in the English Language Specialist Program in the U.S. Department of State's Bureau of Educational and Cultural Affairs.

Allen Ascher

Allen Ascher has been a teacher and teacher trainer in China and the United States, as well as academic director of the intensive English program at Hunter College. Mr. Ascher has also been an ELT publisher and was responsible for publication and expansion of numerous well-known courses including *True Colors, NorthStar,* the *Longman TOEFL Preparation Series,* and the *Longman Academic Writing Series.* He is coauthor of *Summit,* and he wrote the "Teaching Speaking" module of *Teacher Development Interactive,* an online multimedia teacher-training program.

Ms. Saslow and Mr. Ascher are frequent presenters at professional conferences and have been coauthoring courses for teens, adults, and young adults since 2002.

AUTHORS' ACKNOWLEDGMENTS

The authors are indebted to these reviewers, who provided extensive and detailed feedback and suggestions for *Top Notch,* as well as the hundreds of teachers who completed surveys and participated in focus groups.

Manuel Wilson Alvarado Miles, Quito, Ecuador • **Shirley Ando,** Otemae University, Hyogo, Japan • **Vanessa de Andrade,** CCBEU Inter Americano, Curitiba, Brazil • **Miguel Arrazola,** CBA, Santa Cruz, Bolivia • **Mark Barta,** Proficiency School of English, São Paulo, Brazil • **Edwin Bello,** PROULEX, Guadalajara, Mexico • **Mary Blum,** CBA, Cochabamba, Bolivia • **María Elizabeth Boccia,** Proficiency School of English, São Paulo, Brazil • **Pamela Cristina Borja Baltán,** Quito, Ecuador • **Eliana Anabel L. Buccia,** AMICANA, Mendoza, Argentina • **José Humberto Calderón Díaz,** CALUSAC, Guatemala City, Guatemala • **María Teresa Calienes Csirke,** Idiomas Católica, Lima, Peru • **Esther María Carbo Morales,** Quito, Ecuador • **Jorge Washington Cárdenas Castillo,** Quito, Ecuador • **Eréndira Yadira Carrera García,** UVM Chapultepec, Mexico City, Mexico • **Viviane de Cássia Santos Carlini,** Spectrum Line, Pouso Alegre, Brazil • **Centro Colombo Americano,** Bogota, Colombia • **Guven Ciftci,** Fatih University, Istanbul, Turkey • **Diego Cisneros,** CBA, Tarija, Bolivia • **Paul Crook,** Meisei University, Tokyo, Japan • **Alejandra Díaz Loo,** El Cultural, Arequipa, Peru • **Jesús G. Díaz Osío,** Florida National College, Miami, USA • **María Eid Ceneviva,** CBA, Bolivia • **Amalia Elvira Rodríguez Espinoza De Los Monteros,** Guayaquil, Ecuador • **María Argelia Estrada Vásquez,** CALUSAC, Guatemala City, Guatemala • **John Fieldeldy,** College of Engineering, Nihon University, Aizuwakamatsu-shi, Japan • **Marleni Humbelina Flores Urízar,** CALUSAC, Guatemala City, Guatemala • **Gonzalo Fortune,** CBA, Sucre, Bolivia • **Andrea Fredricks,** Embassy CES, San Francisco, USA • **Irma Gallegos Peláez,** UVM Tlalpan, Mexico City, Mexico • **Alberto Gamarra,** CBA, Santa Cruz, Bolivia • **María Amparo García Peña,** ICPNA Cusco, Peru • **Amanda Gillis-Furutaka,** Kyoto Sangyo University, Kyoto, Japan • **Martha Angelina González**

Párraga, Guayaquil, Ecuador • **Octavio Garduño Ruiz,** Business Training Consultant, Mexico City, Mexico • **Ralph Grayson,** Idiomas Católica, Lima, Peru • **Murat Gultekin,** Fatih University, Istanbul, Turkey • **Oswaldo Gutiérrez,** PROULEX, Guadalajara, Mexico • **Ayaka Hashinishi,** Otemae University, Hyogo, Japan • **Alma Lorena Hernández de Armas,** CALUSAC, Guatemala City, Guatemala • **Kent Hill,** Seigakuin University, Saitama-ken, Japan • **Kayoko Hirao,** Nichii Gakkan Company, COCO Juku, Japan • **Jesse Huang,** National Central University, Taoyuan, Taiwan • **Eric Charles Jones,** Seoul University of Technology, Seoul, South Korea • **Jun-Chen Kuo,** Tajen University, Pingtung , Taiwan • **Susan Krieger,** Embassy CES, San Francisco, USA • **Ana María de la Torre Ugarte,** ICPNA Chiclayo, Peru • **Erin Lemaistre,** Chung-Ang University, Seoul, South Korea • **Eleanor S. Leu,** Soochow University, Taipei, Taiwan • **Yihui Li (Stella Li),** Fooyin University, Kaohsiung, Taiwan • **Chin-Fan Lin,** Shih Hsin University, Taipei, Taiwan • **Linda Lin,** Tatung Institute of Technology, Taiwan • **Kristen Lindblom,** Embassy CES, San Francisco, USA • **Patricio David López Logacho,** Quito, Ecuador • **Diego López Tasara,** Idiomas Católica, Lima, Peru • **Neil Macleod,** Kansai Gaidai University, Osaka, Japan • **Adriana Marcés,** Idiomas Católica, Lima, Peru • **Robyn McMurray,** Pusan National University, Busan, South Korea • **Paula Medina,** London Language Institute, London, Canada • **Juan Carlos Muñoz,** American School Way, Bogota, Colombia • **Noriko Mori,** Otemae University, Hyogo, Japan • **Adrián Esteban Narváez Pacheco,** Cuenca, Ecuador • **Tim Newfields,** Tokyo University Faculty of Economics, Tokyo, Japan • **Ana Cristina Ochoa,** CCBEU Inter Americano, Curitiba, Brazil • **Tania Elizabeth Ortega Santacruz,** Cuenca, Ecuador • **Martha Patricia Páez,** Quito, Ecuador • **María de Lourdes Pérez Valdespino,** Universidad del Valle

de México, Mexico • **Wahrena Elizabeth Pfeister,** University of Suwon, Gyeonggi-Do, South Korea • **Wayne Allen Pfeister,** University of Suwon, Gyeonggi-Do, South Korea • **Andrea Rebonato,** CCBEU Inter Americano, Curitiba, Brazil • **Thomas Robb,** Kyoto Sangyo University, Kyoto, Japan • **Mehran Sabet,** Seigakuin University, Saitama-ken, Japan • **Majid Safadaran Mosazadeh,** ICPNA Chiclayo, Peru • **Timothy Samuelson,** BridgeEnglish, Denver, USA • **Héctor Sánchez,** PROULEX, Guadalajara, Mexico • **Mónica Alexandra Sánchez Escalante,** Quito, Ecuador • **Jorge Mauricio Sánchez Montalván,** Quito, Universidad Politécnica Salesiana (UPS), Ecuador • **Letícia Santos,** ICBEU Ibiá, Brazil • **Elena Sapp,** INTO Oregon State University, Corvallis, USA • **Robert Sheridan,** Otemae University, Hyogo, Japan • **John Eric Sherman,** Hong Ik University, Seoul, South Korea • **Brooks Slaybaugh,** Asia University, Tokyo, Japan • **João Vitor Soares,** NACC, São Paulo, Brazil • **Silvia Solares,** CBA, Sucre, Bolivia • **Chayawan Sonchaeng,** Delaware County Community College, Media, PA • **María Julia Suárez,** CBA, Cochabamba, Bolivia • **Elena Sudakova,** English Language Center, Kiev, Ukraine • **Richard Swingle,** Kansai Gaidai College, Osaka, Japan • **Blanca Luz Terrazas Zamora,** ICPNA Cusco, Peru • **Sandrine Ting,** St. John's University, New Taipei City, Taiwan • **Christian Juan Torres Medina,** Guayaquil, Ecuador • **Raquel Torrico,** CBA, Sucre, Bolivia • **Jessica Ueno,** Otemae University, Hyogo, Japan • **Ximena Vacaflor C.,** CBA, Tarija, Bolivia • **René Valdivia Pereira,** CBA, Santa Cruz, Bolivia • **Solange Lopes Vinagre Costa,** SENAC, São Paulo, Brazil • **Magno Alejandro Vivar Hurtado,** Cuenca, Ecuador • **Dr. Wen-hsien Yang,** National Kaohsiung Hospitality College, Kaohsiung, Taiwan • **Juan Zárate,** El Cultural, Arequipa, Peru

LEARNING OBJECTIVES

	COMMUNICATION GOALS	VOCABULARY	GRAMMAR

UNIT 1
Getting Acquainted
PAGE 2
	• Get reacquainted with someone
	• Greet a visitor to your country
	• Discuss gestures and customs
	• Describe an interesting experience
		• Tourist activities
		• The hand
		• Participial adjectives
			• The present perfect
			  ○ Statements and <u>yes</u> / <u>no</u> questions
			  ○ Form and usage
			  ○ Past participles of irregular verbs
			  ○ With <u>already</u>, <u>yet</u>, <u>ever</u>, <u>before</u>, and <u>never</u>
			GRAMMAR BOOSTER
			  • The present perfect
			    ○ Information questions
			    ○ <u>Yet</u> and <u>already</u>: expansion, common errors
			    ○ <u>Ever</u>, <u>never</u>, and <u>before</u>: use and placement

UNIT 2
Going to the Movies
PAGE 14
	• Apologize for being late
	• Discuss preferences for movie genres
	• Describe and recommend movies
	• Discuss effects of movie violence on viewers
		• Explanations for being late
		• Movie genres
		• Adjectives to describe movies
			• The present perfect
			  ○ With <u>for</u> and <u>since</u>
			  ○ Other uses
			• Wants and preferences: <u>would like</u> and <u>would rather</u>
			  ○ Form and usage
			  ○ Statements, questions, and answers
			GRAMMAR BOOSTER
			  • The present perfect continuous
			  • The present participle: spelling
			  • Expressing preferences: review, expansion, and common errors

UNIT 3
Staying in Hotels
PAGE 26
	• Leave and take a message
	• Check into a hotel
	• Request housekeeping services
	• Choose a hotel
		• Hotel room types and kinds of beds
		• Hotel room amenities and services
			• The future with <u>will</u>
			  ○ Form and usage
			  ○ Statements and questions
			  ○ Contractions
			• The real conditional
			  ○ Form and usage
			  ○ Statements and questions
			GRAMMAR BOOSTER
			  • <u>Will</u>: expansion
			  • <u>Can</u>, <u>should</u>, and <u>have to</u>: future meaning
			  • The real conditinal: factual and future; usage and common errors

UNIT 4
Cars and Driving
PAGE 38
	• Discuss a car accident
	• Describe a car problem
	• Rent a car
	• Discuss good and bad driving
		• Bad driving habits
		• Car parts
		• Ways to respond (with concern / relief)
		• Phrasal verbs for talking about cars
		• Car types
		• Driving behavior
			• The past continuous
			  ○ Form and usage
			  ○ Vs. the simple past tense
			• Direct objects with phrasal verbs
			GRAMMAR BOOSTER
			  • The past continuous: other uses
			  • Nouns and pronouns: review

UNIT 5
Personal Care and Appearance
PAGE 50
	• Ask for something in a store
	• Make an appointment at a salon or spa
	• Discuss ways to improve appearance
	• Define the meaning of beauty
		• Salon services
		• Personal care products
		• Discussing beauty
			• Indefinite quantities and amounts
			  ○ <u>Some</u> and <u>any</u>
			  ○ <u>A lot of</u> / <u>lots of</u>, <u>many</u>, and <u>much</u>
			• Indefinite pronouns: <u>someone</u> / <u>no one</u> / <u>anyone</u>
			GRAMMAR BOOSTER
			  • <u>Some</u> and <u>any</u>: indefiniteness
			  • <u>Too many</u>, <u>too much</u>, and <u>enough</u>
			  • Comparative quantifiers <u>fewer</u> and <u>less</u>
			  • Indefinite pronouns: <u>something</u>, <u>anything</u>, and <u>nothing</u>

CONVERSATION STRATEGIES	LISTENING / PRONUNCIATION	READING	WRITING
• Use "I don't think so." to soften a negative answer • Say "I know!" to exclaim that you've discovered an answer • Use "Welcome to ___." to greet someone in a new place • Say "That's great." to acknowledge someone's positive experience	**Listening Skills** • Listen to classify • Listen for details **Pronunciation** • Sound reduction in the present perfect	**Texts** • A poster about world customs • A magazine article about non-verbal communication • A travel poster • A photo story **Skills/strategies** • Identify supporting details • Relate to personal experience	**Task** • Write a description of an interesting experience **WRITING BOOSTER** • Avoiding run-on sentences
• Apologize and provide a reason when late • Say "That's fine." to reassure • Offer to repay someone with "How much do I owe?" • Use "What would you rather do . . . ? to ask about preference • Soften a negative response with "To tell you the truth, . . ."	**Listening Skills** • Listen for main ideas • Listen to infer • Dictation **Pronunciation** • Reduction of h	**Texts** • A movie website • Movie reviews • A textbook excerpt about violence in movies • A photo story **Skills/strategies** • Understand from context • Confirm content • Evaluate ideas	**Task** • Write an essay about violence in movies and on TV **WRITING BOOSTER** • Paragraphs • Topic sentences
• Say "Would you like to leave a message?" if someone isn't available • Say "Let's see." to indicate you're checking information • Make a formal, polite request with "May I ___?" • Say "Here you go." when handing someone something • Use "By the way, . . ." to introduce new information	**Listening Skills** • Listen to take phone messages • Listen for main ideas • Listen for details **Pronunciation** • Contractions with will	**Texts** • Phone message slips • A hotel website • A city map • A photo story **Skills/strategies** • Draw conclusions • Identify supporting details • Interpret a map	**Task** • Write a paragraph explaining the reasons for choosing a hotel **WRITING BOOSTER** • Avoiding sentence fragments with because or since
• Express concern about another's condition after an accident • Express relief when hearing all is OK • Use "only" to minimize the seriousness of a situation • Use "actually" to soften negative information • Empathize with "I'm sorry to hear that."	**Listening Skills** • Listen for details • Listen to summarize **Pronunciation** • Stress of particles in phrasal verbs	**Texts** • A questionnaire about bad driving habits • Rental car customer profiles • A feature article about defensive driving • A driving behavior survey • A photo story **Skills/strategies** • Understand from context • Critical thinking	**Task** • Write a paragraph comparing good and bad drivers **WRITING BOOSTER** • Connecting words and sentences: and, in addition, furthermore, and therefore
• Use "Excuse me." to initiate a conversation with a salesperson • Confirm information by repeating it with rising intonation • Use "No problem." to show you don't mind an inconvenience • Use "Let me check" to ask someone to wait while you confirm information	**Listening Skills** • Listen to recognize someone's point of view • Listen to take notes **Pronunciation** • Pronunciation of unstressed vowels	**Texts** • A spa and fitness center advertisement • A health advice column • A photo story **Skills/strategies** • Paraphrase • Understand from context • Confirm content • Apply information	**Task** • Write a letter on how to improve appearance **WRITING BOOSTER** • Writing a formal letter

	COMMUNICATION GOALS	VOCABULARY	GRAMMAR
UNIT 6 **Eating Well** PAGE 62	• Talk about food passions • Make an excuse to decline food • Discuss lifestyle changes • Describe local dishes	• Nutrition terminology • Food passions • Excuses for not eating something • Food descriptions	• Use to / used to • Negative yes / no questions **GRAMMAR BOOSTER** • Use to / used to: use and form, common errors • Be used to vs. get used to • Repeated actions in the past: would + base form, common errors • Negative yes / no questions: short answers
UNIT 7 **About Personality** PAGE 74	• Get to know a new friend • Cheer someone up • Discuss personality and its origin • Examine the impact of birth order on personality	• Positive and negative adjectives • Terms to discuss psychology and personality	• Gerunds and infinitives • Gerunds as objects of prepositions **GRAMMAR BOOSTER** • Gerunds and infinitives: other uses • Negative gerunds

UNIT 8
The Arts
PAGE 86
	• Recommend a museum
	• Ask about and describe objects
	• Talk about artistic talent
	• Discuss your favorite artists
		• Kinds of art
		• Adjectives to describe art
		• Objects, handicrafts, and materials
		• Passive participial phrases
			• The passive voice
			  ○ Form, meaning, and usage
			  ○ Statements and questions
			
			GRAMMAR BOOSTER
			• Transitive and intransitive verbs
			• The passive voice: other tenses
			• Yes / no questions in the passive voice: other tenses

UNIT 9
Living in Cyberspace
PAGE 98
	• Troubleshoot a problem
	• Compare product features
	• Describe how you use the Internet
	• Discuss the impact of the Internet
		• Ways to reassure someone
		• The computer screen, components, and commands
		• Internet activities
			• The infinitive of purpose
			• Comparisons with as . . . as
			  ○ Meaning and usage
			  ○ Just, almost, not quite, not nearly
			
			GRAMMAR BOOSTER
			• Expressing purpose with in order to and for
			• As . . . as to compare adverbs
			• Comparatives / superlatives: review
			• Comparison with adverbs

UNIT 10
Ethics and Values
PAGE 110
	• Discuss ethical choices
	• Return someone else's property
	• Express personal values
	• Discuss acts of kindness and honesty
		• Idioms
		• Situations that require an ethical choice
		• Acknowledging thanks
		• Personal values
			• The unreal conditional
			  ○ Form, usage, common errors
			• Possessive pronouns / Whose
			  ○ Form, usage, common errors
			
			GRAMMAR BOOSTER
			• should, ought to, had better
			• have to, must, be supposed to
			• Possessive nouns: review and expansion
			• Pronouns: summary

CONVERSATION STRATEGIES	LISTENING / PRONUNCIATION	READING	WRITING
• Provide an emphatic affirmative response with "Definitely." • Offer food with "Please help yourself." • Acknowledge someone's efforts by saying something positive • Soften the rejection of an offer with "I'll pass on the ___." • Use a negative question to express surprise • Use "It's not a problem." to downplay inconvenience	**Listening Skills** • Listen for details • Listen to personalize **Pronunciation** • Sound reduction: <u>used to</u>	**Texts** • A food guide • Descriptions of types of diets • A magazine article about eating habits • A lifestyle survey • Menu ingredients • A photo story **Skills/strategies** • Understand from context • Summarize • Compare and contrast	**Task** • Write a persuasive paragraph about the differences in present-day and past diets **WRITING BOOSTER** • Connecting ideas: subordinating conjunctions
• Clarify an earlier question with "Well, for example, . . ." • Buy time to think with "Let's see." • Use auxiliary <u>do</u> to emphasize a verb • Thank someone for showing interest. • Offer empathy with "I know what you mean."	**Listening Skills** • Listen for main ideas • Listen for specific information • Classify information • Infer information **Pronunciation** • Reduction of <u>to</u> in infinitives	**Texts** • A pop psychology website • A textbook excerpt about the nature / nurture controversy • Personality surveys • A photo story **Skills/strategies** • Understand vocabulary from context • Make personal comparisons	**Task** • Write an essay describing someone's personality **WRITING BOOSTER** • Parallel structure
• Say "Be sure not to miss ___." to emphasize the importance of an action • Introduce the first aspect of an opinion with "For one thing, . . ." • Express enthusiasm for what someone has said with "No kidding!" • Invite someone's opinion with "What do you think of ___?"	**Listening Skills** • Understand from context • Listen to take notes • Infer point of view **Pronunciation** • Emphatic stress	**Texts** • Museum descriptions • A book excerpt about the origin of artistic talent • An artistic survey • A photo story **Skills/strategies** • Recognize the main idea • Identify supporting details • Paraphrase	**Task** • Write a detailed description of a decorative object **WRITING BOOSTER** • Providing supporting details
• Ask for assistance with "Could you take a look at ___?" • Introduce an explanation with "Well, . . ." • Make a suggestion with "Why don't you try ___ing?" • Express interest informally with "Oh, yeah?" • Use "Everyone says . . ." to introduce a popular opinion • Say "Well, I've heard ___." to support a point of view	**Listening Skills** • Listen for the main idea • Listen for details **Pronunciation** • Stress in <u>as</u> . . . <u>as</u> phrases	**Texts** • A social network website • An internet user survey • Newspaper clippings about the Internet • A photo story **Skills/strategies** • Understand from context • Relate to personal experience	**Task** • Write an essay evaluating the benefits and problems of the Internet **WRITING BOOSTER** • Organizing ideas
• Say "You think so?" to reconfirm someone's opinion • Provide an emphatic affirmative response with "Absolutely." • Acknowledge thanks with "Don't mention it."	**Listening Skills** • Listen to infer information • Listen for main ideas • Understand vocabulary from context • Support ideas with details **Pronunciation** • Blending of <u>d + y</u> in <u>would you</u>	**Texts** • A personal values self-test • Print and online news stories about kindness and honesty • A photo story **Skills/strategies** • Summarize • Interpret information • Relate to personal experience	**Task** • Write an essay about someone's personal choice **WRITING BOOSTER** • Introducing conflicting ideas: <u>On the one hand</u>; <u>On the other hand</u>

TO THE TEACHER

What is *Top Notch*?
Top Notch is a six-level* communicative course that prepares adults and young adults to interact successfully and confidently with both native and non-native speakers of English.

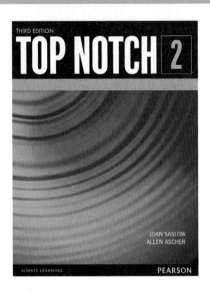

The goal of *Top Notch* is to make English unforgettable through:
- Multiple exposures to new language
- Numerous opportunities to practice it
- Deliberate and intensive recycling

The *Top Notch* course has two beginning levels—*Top Notch Fundamentals* for true beginners and *Top Notch 1* for false beginners. *Top Notch* is benchmarked to the Global Scale of English and is tightly correlated to the Can-do Statements of the Common European Framework of Reference.

Each full level of *Top Notch* contains material for 60–90 hours of classroom instruction. In addition, the entire course can be tailored to blended learning with an integrated online component, *MyEnglishLab*.

NEW This third edition of *Top Notch* includes these new features: Extra Grammar Exercises, digital full-color Vocabulary Flash Cards, Conversation Activator videos, and Pronunciation Coach videos.

* Summit 1 and *Summit 2* are the titles of the 5th and 6th levels of the *Top Notch* course.

Award-Winning Instructional Design*

Daily confirmation of progress

Each easy-to-follow two-page lesson begins with a clearly stated practical communication goal closely aligned to the Common European Framework's Can-do Statements. All activities are integrated with the goal, giving vocabulary and grammar meaning and purpose. *Now You Can* activities ensure that students achieve each goal and confirm their progress in every class session.

Explicit vocabulary and grammar

Clear captioned picture-dictionary illustrations with accompanying audio take the guesswork out of meaning and pronunciation. Grammar presentations containing both rules and examples clarify form, meaning, and use. The unique *Recycle this Language* feature continually puts known words and grammar in front of students' eyes as they communicate, to make sure language remains active.

High-frequency social language

Twenty memorable conversation models provide appealing natural social language that students can carry "in their pockets" for use in real life. Rigorous controlled and free discussion activities systematically stimulate recycling of social language, ensuring that it's not forgotten.

Linguistic and cultural fluency

Top Notch equips students to interact with people from different language backgrounds by including authentic accents on the audio. Conversation Models, Photo Stories, and cultural fluency activities prepare students for social interactions in English with people from unfamiliar cultures.

Active listening syllabus

All Vocabulary presentations, Pronunciation presentations, Conversation Models, Photo Stories, Listening Comprehension exercises, and Readings are recorded on the audio to help students develop good pronunciation, intonation, and auditory memory. In addition, approximately fifty carefully developed listening tasks at each level of *Top Notch* develop crucial listening comprehension skills such as listen for details, listen for main ideas, listen to activate vocabulary, listen to activate grammar, and listen to confirm information.

*We wish you and your students enjoyment and success with **Top Notch 2**.
We wrote it for you.*

Joan Saslow and Allen Ascher

** **Top Notch** is the recipient of the Association of Educational Publishers' Distinguished Achievement Award.*

COMPONENTS

ActiveTeach

Maximize the impact of your *Top Notch* lessons. This digital tool provides an interactive classroom experience that can be used with or without an interactive whiteboard (IWB). It includes a full array of digital and printable features.

For class presentation . . .

 NEW Conversation Activator videos: increase students' confidence in oral communication

 NEW Pronunciation Coach videos: facilitate clear and fluent oral expression

 NEW Extra Grammar Exercises: ensure mastery of grammar

 NEW Digital Full-Color Flash Cards: accelerate retention of new vocabulary

PLUS

- ▶ Clickable Audio: instant access to the complete classroom audio program
- *Top Notch TV* Video Program: a hilarious sitcom and authentic on-the-street interviews
- *Top Notch Pop and Karaoke*: original songs for additional language practice

For planning . . .

- A *Methods Handbook* for a communicative classroom
- Detailed timed lesson plans for each two-page lesson
- *Top Notch TV* teaching notes
- Complete answer keys, audio scripts, and video scripts

For extra support . . .

- Hundreds of extra printable activities, with teaching notes
- *Top Notch Pop* language exercises
- *Top Notch TV* activity worksheets

For assessment . . .

- Ready-made unit and review Achievement Tests with options to edit, add, or delete items.

MyEnglishLab

An optional online learning tool

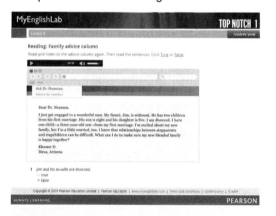

- **NEW** Grammar Coach videos, plus the Pronunciation Coach videos, and Digital Vocabulary Flash Cards
- **NEW** Immediate and meaningful feedback on wrong answers
- **NEW** Remedial grammar exercises
- Interactive practice of all material presented in the course
- Grade reports that display performance and time on task
- Auto-graded Achievement Tests

Workbook

Lesson-by-lesson written exercises to accompany the Student's Book

Full-Course Placement Tests

Choose printable or online version

Classroom Audio Program

- A set of Audio CDs, as an alternative to the clickable audio in the ActiveTeach
- Contains a variety of authentic regional and non-native accents to build comprehension of diverse English speakers
- **NEW** A downloadable Audio App for students allows access anytime, anywhere

Teacher's Edition and Lesson Planner

- Detailed interleaved lesson plans, language and culture notes, answer keys, and more
- Includes ActiveTeach on DVD-ROM, with hundreds of extra printable activities

UNIT 6 — Eating Well

PREVIEW

COMMUNICATION GOALS

1 Talk about food passions.
2 Make an excuse to decline food.
3 Discuss lifestyle changes.
4 Describe local dishes.

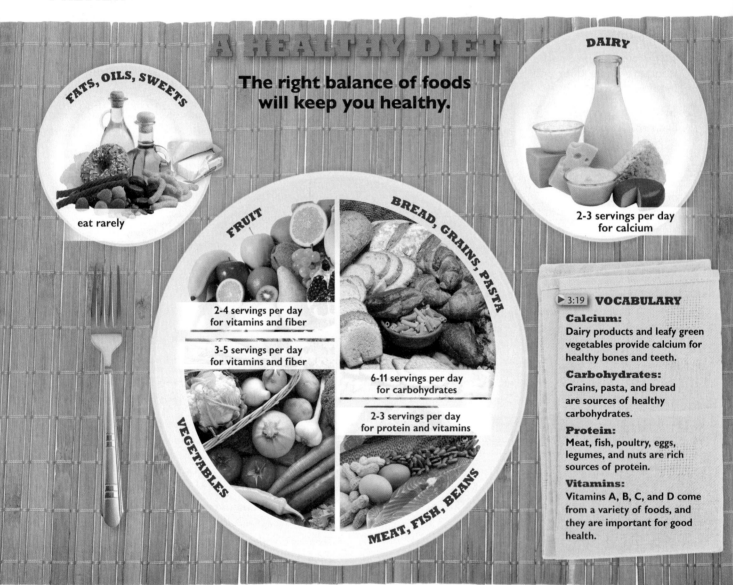

A HEALTHY DIET

The right balance of foods will keep you healthy.

FATS, OILS, SWEETS
eat rarely

DAIRY
2-3 servings per day
for calcium

FRUIT
2-4 servings per day
for vitamins and fiber

3-5 servings per day
for vitamins and fiber

VEGETABLES

BREAD, GRAINS, PASTA
6-11 servings per day
for carbohydrates

2-3 servings per day
for protein and vitamins

MEAT, FISH, BEANS

▶ 3:19 **VOCABULARY**

Calcium:
Dairy products and leafy green vegetables provide calcium for healthy bones and teeth.

Carbohydrates:
Grains, pasta, and bread are sources of healthy carbohydrates.

Protein:
Meat, fish, poultry, eggs, legumes, and nuts are rich sources of protein.

Vitamins:
Vitamins A, B, C, and D come from a variety of foods, and they are important for good health.

A   Look at the suggestions above for eating a healthy diet. Do you think this diet is healthy? Why or why not?

B   Complete the chart about the foods you eat each day. Compare charts with a partner.

C   **DISCUSSION**   How are the Healthy Diet suggestions different from your chart? Which do you think is a healthier diet? Explain.

2–3 servings a day
3–5 servings a day
More than 5 servings a day

▶ 3:20 **PHOTO STORY** Read and listen to people talking about food choices.

Rita: Didn't you tell me you were avoiding sweets?

Joy: I couldn't resist! I had a craving for chocolate.

Rita: Well, I have to admit it looks pretty good. How many calories are in that thing anyway?

Joy: I have no idea. Want to try some?

Rita: Thanks. But I think I'd better pass. I'm avoiding carbs.*

Joy: You? I don't believe it. You never used to turn down chocolate!

Rita: I know. But I'm watching my weight now.

Joy: Come on! It's really good.

Rita: OK. Maybe just a bite.

Joy: Hey, you only live once!

*carbs (informal) = carbohydrates

E **FOCUS ON LANGUAGE** Find an underlined sentence or phrase in the Photo Story with the same meaning as each of the following.

1 I don't know. ....

2 I should say no. ....

3 I couldn't stop myself. ....

4 I'm trying not to get heavier. ....

5 I really wanted . . . .

6 I agree . . . .

7 say no to ....

8 I'll try a little. ....

SPEAKING

Read the descriptions of diets. Would you ever try any of them? Why or why not?

> " I don't believe in the Atkins Diet. A lot of meat, eggs, and cheese doesn't sound like the right balance of foods for good health. "

The Mushroom Diet
For weight loss.
Replace lunch or dinner every day—for two weeks— with a mushroom dish.

The Vegan Diet
For better health and prevention of disease.
Avoid all animal products, including dairy and eggs. Eat lots of grains, beans, vegetables, and fruits.

The Atkins Diet
For weight loss.
Eat high-protein foods such as meat, eggs, and cheese. Avoid foods that are high in carbohydrates, such as potatoes, bread, grains, and sugar.

The Juice Fast
For better health and prevention of disease.
Instead of food, drink four to six glasses of fresh vegetable and fruit juices for anywhere from three days to three weeks. Get plenty of rest and avoid exercise during the fast.

GOAL Talk about food passions

VOCABULARY *Food passions*

DIGITAL FLASH CARDS

A ▶3:21 Read and listen. Then listen again and repeat.

I'm **crazy about** seafood.
I'm **a big** meat **eater**.
I'm **a big** coffee **drinker**.
I'm **a chocolate addict**.
I'm **a pizza lover**.

I **can't stand** fish.
I'm **not crazy about** chocolate.
I **don't care for** steak.
I'm **not much of a** pizza **eater**.
I'm **not much of a** coffee **drinker**.

B ▶3:22 **LISTEN TO ACTIVATE VOCABULARY** Circle the correct words to complete each statement about the speakers' food passions.

1 She (is crazy about / doesn't care for) sushi.

2 He (loves / can't stand) asparagus.

3 She (is a mango lover / doesn't care for mangoes).

4 He (is a big pasta eater / isn't crazy about pasta).

5 She (is an ice cream addict / can't stand ice cream).

sushi

mangoes

pasta

ice cream

asparagus

C **PAIR WORK** Tell your partner about some of your food passions.

I'm really a seafood lover, but I'm not crazy about clams.

GRAMMAR *Use to / used to*

Use use to and used to + the base form of a verb to describe things that were true in the past but are no longer true in the present.

I **used to be** crazy about candy, but now I don't care for it.
She **didn't use to eat** cheese, but now she has it all the time.

Did you **use to eat** a lot of fatty foods? | Yes, I did. | OR | Yes, I used to.
| No, I didn't. | | No, I didn't use to.

What **did** you **use to have** for breakfast? (Eggs and sausage. But not anymore.)
Why **did** you **use to eat** so much? (Because I didn't use to worry about my health.)

Be careful!

They **used** to . . . BUT | They didn't **use** to . . .
| Did they **use** to . . . ?

GRAMMAR BOOSTER p. 134
• Use to / used to: use and form, common errors
• Be used to vs. get used to
• Repeated actions in the past: would + base form, common errors

GRAMMAR PRACTICE Use the context to help you complete each sentence with <u>used to</u> or <u>didn't use to</u>. Then write two sentences about yourself.

1 Gary .... go out to eat a lot, but now he eats at home more often.

2 Nina .... eat a lot of pasta, but now she does.

3 Vinnie .... drink a lot of coffee, but now he's a coffee addict.

4 Anton .... eat a lot of vegetables, but now he doesn't.

5 Cate .... hate seafood, but now she's crazy about fish.

6 Ted .... eat a lot of fatty foods, but now he avoids them.

7 Burt .... drink a lot of water, but now he has several glasses a day.

8 May .... like salad, but now she has salads several times a week.

9 (used to) I ....
....

10 (didn't use to) I ....
....

DIGITAL
MORE
EXERCISES

DIGITAL
VIDEO
COACH

PRONUNCIATION *Sound reduction:* <u>used to</u>

▶3:23 Notice how the pronunciation of <u>to</u> in <u>used to</u> changes to /tə/ in natural speech. Read and listen. Then listen again and repeat. Practice the sentences on your own.

1 I used to be a big meat eater.

2 Jack used to like sweets.

3 Sally used to be crazy about fries.

4 They didn't use to like seafood.

CONVERSATION MODEL

A ▶3:24 Read and listen to two people talking about their food passions.

A: Are you a big coffee drinker?

B: Definitely. I'm crazy about coffee. What about you?

A: I used to drink it a lot. But recently I've cut back.

B: Well, I couldn't live without it.

B ▶3:25 **RHYTHM AND INTONATION** Listen again and repeat. Then practice the Conversation Model with a partner.

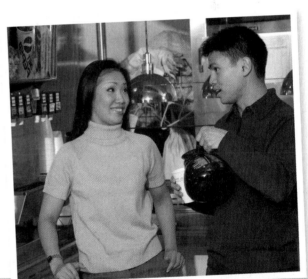

NOW YOU CAN Talk about food passions

A **NOTEPADDING** Complete the notepad with foods you like and dislike.

DIGITAL
VIDEO

B **CONVERSATION ACTIVATOR** With a partner, change the Conversation Model, exchanging information about your food passions. Talk about what you used to and didn't use to eat or drink. Use your notepad and the Vocabulary from page 64.

A: Are you a big .... ?
B: .... What about you?
A: ....

DON'T STOP!
• Ask about more foods and drinks.

My food passions	
Foods I'm crazy about	Foods I can't stand

C **CHANGE PARTNERS** Talk about other food passions.

GOAL Make an excuse to decline food

CONVERSATION MODEL

A ▶3:26 Read and listen to a dinner guest make an excuse to decline food.

A: Please help yourself.

B: Everything looks great! But I'll pass on the chicken.

A: Don't you eat chicken?

B: Actually, no. I'm a vegetarian.

A: I'm sorry. I didn't know that.

B: It's not a problem. I'll have something else.

B ▶3:27 **RHYTHM AND INTONATION** Listen again and repeat. Then practice the Conversation Model with a partner.

▶3:28 **Variations**
It's not a problem.
Don't worry.
I'm fine.

VOCABULARY *Excuses for not eating something*

DIGITAL FLASH CARDS

A ▶3:29 Read and listen. Then listen again and repeat.

Coffee **doesn't agree with me**.

I'm **on a diet**. / I'm **trying to lose weight**.

I don't eat beef. It's **against my religion**.

I'm **allergic to** chocolate.

I'm **avoiding** sugar.

I **don't care for** broccoli.

B ▶3:30 **LISTEN TO ACTIVATE VOCABULARY** Listen to each conversation. Write the letter to complete each statement. Then listen again to check your work.

.... 1 Cindy . . .   **a** is a vegetarian.

.... 2 Frankie . . .   **b** is avoiding fatty, salty foods.

.... 3 Marie . . .   **c** is trying to lose weight.

.... 4 Susan . . .   **d** is allergic to something.

.... 5 George . . .   **e** doesn't care for seafood.

C **PAIR WORK** Talk about foods or drinks you avoid. Explain why.

❝ I usually don't eat fried foods. I'm trying to lose weight. ❞

GRAMMAR *Negative yes / no questions*

Use negative yes / no questions . . .
- **to confirm information you think is true.**
  Isn't Jane a vegetarian? (Yes, she is.)
  Didn't he go on a diet last week? (Yes. He's trying the Atkins Diet.)
- **when you want someone to agree with you.**
  Don't you love Italian food? (Yes, it's delicious!)
  Wasn't that a terrible dinner? (Actually, no. I thought it was good.)
- **to express surprise.**
  Aren't you going to have cake? (I'm sorry, but I'm on a diet.)
  Hasn't he tried the chicken? (No. He's a vegetarian.)

> **GRAMMAR BOOSTER** p. 135
> - Negative yes / no
>   questions: short answers

GRAMMAR PRACTICE Complete each negative yes / no question.

1 A: .... you allergic to tomatoes?
   B: Me? No. You're thinking of my brother.

2 A: .... that lunch yesterday delicious?
   B: It was fantastic!

3 A: .... we already have steak this week?
   B: Yes, we did.

4 A: .... your husband been on a diet?
   B: Yes. But it's driving him crazy.

5 A: .... asparagus disgusting?
   B: Actually, I like it.

6 A: .... you like your pasta?
   B: Actually, it was a little too spicy for me.

NOW YOU CAN Make an excuse to decline food

A **NOTEPADDING** Look at the photos. On a separate sheet of paper, use the Vocabulary to write an excuse to decline each food.

B **CONVERSATION ACTIVATOR** With a partner, change the Conversation Model to role-play a dinner conversation. Use the photos to offer foods. Use your notepad to make excuses to decline that food. Then change roles. OPTION: Role-play a dinner conversation with more than one classmate.

A: Please help yourself.
B: Everything looks .... ! But I'll pass on the ....
A: Don't you eat .... ?
B: Actually, ...
A: I'm sorry. I didn't know that.
B: .... I'll have ....

DON'T STOP!
- Offer drinks and other foods.
- Talk about food passions.

RECYCLE THIS LANGUAGE.

be crazy about __	can't stand __
be a big __ eater / drinker	be not crazy about __
be a(n) __ addict / lover	not care for __

C **CHANGE PARTNERS** Practice the conversation again.

octopus

shellfish

tofu

steak

broccoli   beets

chocolate

GOAL Discuss lifestyle changes

BEFORE YOU READ

EXPLORE YOUR IDEAS Do you think people's eating habits are better or worse than they used to be? Explain with examples.

READING ▶3:31

How Can It Be?
Americans gain weight ... while the French stay thin

Have you ever wondered why Americans struggle with watching their weight, while the French, who consume all that rich food—the bread, the cheese, the wine, and the heavy sauces—continue to stay thin? Now a report from Cornell University suggests a possible answer. A study of almost 300 participants from France and the U.S. provides clues about how lifestyle and decisions about eating may affect weight. Researchers concluded that the French tend to stop eating when they feel full. However, Americans tend to stop when their plate is completely empty, or they have reached the end of their favorite TV show.

According to Dr. Joseph Mercola, who writes extensively about health issues, the French see eating as an important part of their lifestyle. They enjoy food and, therefore, spend a fairly long time at the table. In contrast, Americans see eating as something to do quickly as they squeeze meals between the other activities of the day. Mercola believes Americans have lost the ability to sense when they are actually full. So they keep eating long after the French would have stopped. In addition, he argues that, by tradition, the French tend to shop daily, walking to small shops and farmers' markets where they have a choice of fresh fruits, vegetables, and eggs as well as high-quality meats and cheeses for each meal. In contrast, Americans tend to drive their cars to huge supermarkets to buy canned and frozen foods for the whole week.

Despite all these differences, new reports show that recent lifestyle changes may be affecting French eating habits. Today, the rate of obesity—or extreme overweight—among adults is only 6%. However, as American fast-food restaurants gain acceptance, and the young turn their backs on older traditions, the obesity rate among French children has reached 17%—and is growing.

A **UNDERSTAND FROM CONTEXT** Use the context of the article to help you choose the same meaning as each underlined word or phrase.

1 Have you ever wondered why Americans <u>struggle with</u> watching their weight . . .
   a have an easy time   **b** have a difficult time   **c** don't care about

2 . . . while the French, who consume all that <u>rich food</u>, ...
   a fatty, high-calorie food   **b** low-fat, low-calorie food   **c** expensive food

3 . . . continue to <u>stay thin</u>?
   a worry about their weight   **b** not become overweight   **c** gain weight

4 Researchers concluded that the French tend to stop eating when they feel <u>full</u>.
   a like they can't eat any more   **b** worried about their weight   **c** hungry

5 . . . the French see eating as an important part of their <u>lifestyle</u>.
   a personal care and appearance   **b** culture or daily routine   **c** meals

B   **SUMMARIZE**   According to the article, why do the French stay thin while Americans gain weight? Write a four-sentence summary of the Reading. Then share your summary with the class.

> Compared to Americans, the French stay thin because . . .

C   **COMPARE AND CONTRAST**   In your country, do people generally stay thin or do they struggle with watching their weight? Are lifestyles in your country closer to those of France or the U.S., as described in the article?

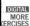

> 66 I think people here are more like people in France. They like to eat, but they don't gain weight easily. 99

NOW YOU CAN Discuss lifestyle changes

A   **FRAME YOUR IDEAS**   Complete the lifestyle self-assessment.

1   Have you ever changed the way you eat in order to lose weight?   ● yes   ● no

If so, what have you done?

○ ate less food   Were you successful?   ○ yes   ○ no

○ cut back on desserts   Why or why not? Explain. _____

○ avoided fatty foods   _____

○ other (explain) _____

2   Have you ever changed the way you eat in order to avoid illness?   ● yes   ● no

If so, what changes have you made?

○ stopped eating fast foods   Were you successful?   ○ yes   ○ no

○ started eating whole grains   Why or why not? Explain. _____

○ started eating more vegetables   _____

○ other (explain) _____

3   Have you ever tried to lead a more active lifestyle?   ● yes   ● no

If so, what have you done?

○ started working out in a gym   Were you successful?   ○ yes   ○ no

○ started running or walking   Why or why not? Explain. _____

○ started playing sports   _____

○ other (explain) _____

B   **CLASS SURVEY**   On the board, summarize your class's lifestyles.

C   **DISCUSSION**   How do you think your classmates compare to most people in your country? Are they generally healthier or less healthy? What do you think people need to do to have a healthy lifestyle?

> 66 I think my classmates are healthier than most people in this country. Too many people eat fast foods. They need to eat healthier food and exercise more. 99

How many students . . .
- want to make some lifestyle changes?
- have gone on a diet to lose weight?
- have changed their diet to improve their health?
- have been successful with a diet?
- lead an active lifestyle?

Text-mining (optional)
Find and underline three words or phrases in the Reading that were new to you. Use them in your Discussion.
    For example: "gain weight."

GOAL Describe local dishes

BEFORE YOU LISTEN

DIGITAL FLASH CARDS

A ▶3:32 **VOCABULARY • *Food descriptions*** Read and listen. Then listen again and repeat.

It looks terrific.

It smells terrible.

It tastes {
sweet.
spicy.
salty.
sour.
}

It smells like
It tastes like } chicken.
It looks like

It's {
soft.
hard.
}

It's {
chewy.
crunchy.
}

B **PAIR WORK** Use the Vocabulary to describe foods you know.

❝ Apples are crunchy. ❞

LISTENING COMPREHENSION

f

cabbage

kim chee / Korea

A ▶3:33 **LISTEN FOR DETAILS** First, listen to the descriptions of foods from around the world and write the letter of each food. Then listen again and choose the Vocabulary that completes each description.

...c.... **1** It's (crunchy / chewy / hard), and it tastes (salty / sweet / sour).

.... **2** It tastes (salty / sweet / spicy), and it's (soft / hard / crunchy).

.... **3** It's (soft / chewy / crunchy), and it tastes (salty / sweet / spicy).

.... **4** It tastes (salty / sweet / spicy). Some think it (tastes / smells / looks) awful.

.... **5** It (smells / tastes / looks) great, and it (smells / tastes / looks) awful.

.... **6** They're (crunchy / chewy / hard), and they taste (salty / sweet / spicy).

e

caviar / Russia

a

chapulines / Mexico

grasshopper

b

cho dofu / China

c

mochi / Japan

d

Jell-O ® / United States

B ▶3:34 **LISTEN TO PERSONALIZE** Listen again. After each food, discuss with a partner whether you would like to try that food. Explain why or why not.

Describe local dishes

A **FRAME YOUR IDEAS** Choose three local dishes that you would recommend to a visitor to your country. Write notes about each.

Name of dish:
Rain doughnuts

Description:
soft and sweet

What's in it?
flour, eggs, milk

Name of dish:

Description:

What's in it?

1

Name of dish:

Description:

What's in it?

3

Name of dish:

Description:

What's in it?

2

B **PAIR WORK** Role-play a conversation in which one of you is a visitor to your country. Introduce and describe your dishes to the "visitor." Use the Vocabulary. For example:

❝ Have you tried rain doughnuts? ❞

❝ No, I haven't. What are they like? ❞

❝ Well, they're soft. And they taste sweet . . . ❞

"rain doughnuts" / Brazil

RECYCLE THIS LANGUAGE.

Ask about the dish	Comment on the dish	
What's in [it / them]?	It sounds / they sound [great].	I'm allergic to __.
Is it / Are they [spicy / sweet]?	I'm crazy about __.	I'm avoiding __.
How do you make [it / them]?	I'm a big __ eater.	__ [don't / doesn't] agree with me.
Is it / Are they [popular]?	I'm a(n) __ [addict / lover].	__ [is / are] against my religion.
Does it / Do they taste [salty]?	I used to / didn't use to] eat __.	I'm not much of a __ [eater].
	I don't care for __.	I'm [on a diet / trying to lose weight].

A ▶3:35 Listen to the conversation in a restaurant. Cross out the foods that the speakers don't mention.

beef and broccoli	chicken	clams	noodles	pasta
pizza	salmon	scallops	shrimp	steak

B ▶3:36 Now listen again and complete the statements.

The man doesn't care for ....

He would rather eat ....

C Complete the negative <u>yes</u> / <u>no</u> question for each situation.

1 The weather today is sunny and beautiful. You turn to your friend and say: "................ the weather fantastic?"

2 You've just finished dinner. It was a terrible meal. As you leave, you say to your friend: "................ that meal awful?"

3 You're sightseeing in China. From your tour bus window you see a long wall in the distance. You say to the person sitting next to you: "................ that the Great Wall?"

4 You're surprised to see your friend eating breakfast at 11:30. You say: "................ you .... breakfast yet?"

5 You see a woman on the street. You're pretty sure it's Norah Jones, the singer. You go up to her and ask: "................ you Norah Jones?"

D Write five sentences about things you used to or didn't use to do or think when you were younger. For example:

> I didn't use to like coffee when I was younger.

E Write short descriptions of the following foods.

apples	bananas	carrots	grapefruit
ice cream	onions	squid	steak

> Carrots are orange, and they're sweet and crunchy.

For additional language practice . . .

♫ TOP NOTCH **POP** • Lyrics p. 154
"A Perfect Dish"

DIGITAL SONG   DIGITAL KARAOKE

WRITING

Write a paragraph on the following topic: Do you think people are eating healthier or less healthy foods than they used to? Give examples to support your opinion.

> I think people are eating a lot of unhealthy foods today.
>
> People used to eat a lot of fresh foods. However, lately . . .

WRITING BOOSTER p. 148
• Connecting ideas: subordinating conjunctions
• Guidance for this writing exercise

International Buffet
Today's Selections

Pad Thai • Thailand

Ingredients: rice noodles, tofu, peanuts, fish sauce, sugar, lime juice, vegetable oil, garlic, shrimp, eggs, hot peppers

Bi Bim Bop • Korea

Ingredients: rice, beef, soy sauce, sesame oil, garlic, black pepper, salt, eggs, lettuce, rice wine, hot peppers

Chicken Mole • Mexico

Ingredients: chicken, salt, vegetable oil, onions, garlic, tomatoes, chocolate, hot peppers

Potato Soup • Colombia

Ingredients: chicken, three kinds of potatoes, corn, avocados

Tabouleh Salad • Lebanon

Ingredients: parsley, mint, onions, tomatoes, salt, black pepper, cracked wheat, lemon juice, olive oil

Pot Stickers • China

Ingredients: flour, cabbage, pork, green onions, sesame oil, salt

Stuffed Rocoto Peppers • Peru

Ingredients: onions, garlic, ground beef, hard-boiled eggs, raisins, cheese, rocoto peppers, vegetable oil

ORAL REVIEW

CHALLENGE Choose a dish and study the photo and the ingredients for one minute. Then close your book. Describe the dish.

PAIR WORK

1 Create a conversation for the man and woman in which they look at the foods and talk about their food passions. For example:

Have you tried Pad Thai? It's terrific!

2 Create a conversation in which the man or the woman suggests and offers foods. The other makes excuses. Start like this:

A: *Would you like some __?*
B: *Actually, __.*

3 Choose a dish and create a conversation between someone from that country and a visitor. For example:

Have you ever tried __?

NOW I CAN

- ☐ Talk about food passions.
- ☐ Make an excuse to decline food.
- ☐ Discuss lifestyle changes.
- ☐ Describe local dishes.

COMMUNICATION GOALS
1 Get to know a new friend.
2 Cheer someone up.
3 Discuss personality and its origin.
4 Examine the impact of birth order.

PREVIEW

The **Psychology** of Color

According to research, colors have a powerful effect on us. Take the test and then see if your answers are confirmed by the research. You may be surprised! (Check your answers below.)

Color test

1) What color is the most attention-getting?

● black   ○ yellow   ● red   ○ other

2) What color is most likely to make people feel angry?

● black   ○ yellow   ● pink   ○ other

3) What color is best for a hospital room?

● pink   ○ white   ● green   ○ other

4) What color often makes people feel tired?

● green   ● blue   ● pink   ○ other

5) What is the least appealing color for food?

● black   ○ yellow   ● blue   ○ other

Answers

1) Experts say red attracts the most attention. Using red for traffic lights and warning lights makes them more noticeable.

2) Studies have shown that being in a yellow room makes it more likely for adults to lose their tempers and for babies to cry.

3) Green is the easiest color on the eye, and it causes people to relax. Painting a hospital room green helps patients get the rest they need.

4) Research has shown that looking at pink can cause people to feel tired. Some sports teams have painted the dressing room of the opposing team pink to reduce the players' energy.

5) Researchers in marketing have found that using blue in processed foods is unappealing. They believe that this is because blue is rare in nature. Painting a restaurant red, on the other hand, increases the appetite. Many restaurants are painted red.

Questionnaire

What are your color preferences?
Look at the colors below.

YELLOW-GREEN
EMERALD GREEN
BRIGHT ORANGE
DARK GRAY
LIGHT BLUE
TOMATO RED
LILAC

Which color do you find the most appealing?

Which color do you most associate with happiness?

Which color do you most associate with being sad?

A   **CLASS SURVEY** How many classmates answered the questions on the test correctly? Which color on the questionnaire was the most appealing to your classmates?

B   **DISCUSSION** In your opinion, what makes people like some colors and dislike others?

❝ I think people like colors that remind them of things they like. ❞

❝ I agree. I love blue. It reminds me of the sky. I love being outdoors. ❞

C ▶4:02 **PHOTO STORY** Read and listen to a couple talking about what color to repaint their living room.

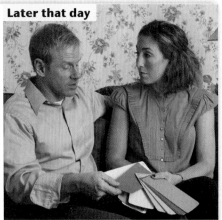

Later that day

Chelsea: You know what? I'm getting a little tired of looking at this wallpaper.

Chad: Well, maybe it's time for a change. What would you think about getting the room painted? I never loved that wallpaper, anyway.

Chelsea: Actually, I don't think either of us did. We only got it because we couldn't agree on a paint color.

Chad: Oh, yeah. Now I remember. You wanted pink, and I said it was too feminine.

Chelsea: Actually, I never thought it was pink. To me it was a soft rose.

Chad: Well, what would you say to a nice blue?

Chelsea: Blue? *Way* too masculine.

Chad: *What?!*

Chelsea: I'm just pulling your leg, silly! Blue would be great.

Chad: This one's nice—very relaxing.

Chelsea: True, but I'm not sure the furniture would go with it.

Chad: Good point. I'd hate to have to get all new stuff . . . You know, maybe we're on the wrong track.

Chelsea: What do you mean?

Chad: All of a sudden, I'm thinking white. It's classic, and . . .

Chelsea: And it goes with everything!

D **PARAPHRASE** Restate the expressions from the Photo Story in your own way.

1 "I'm just pulling your leg."

2 "I'm not sure the furniture would go with it."

3 "Good point."

4 "Maybe we're on the wrong track."

E **THINK AND EXPLAIN** All the statements are false. Explain how you know they are false.

1 Chelsea still likes the wallpaper.

> 💬 Chelsea says, 'I'm getting a little tired of looking at this wallpaper.' 💬

2 Chelsea didn't want a rose-colored living room.

3 Chelsea truly thinks that blue is too masculine.

4 Chelsea thinks the blue Chad likes would go nicely with the furniture.

5 Chad would like to buy new furniture.

6 It's Chelsea's idea to paint the living room white.

7 They agree the furniture wouldn't go with white.

SPEAKING

Choose colors for rooms. Use the Color Test for ideas. Compare charts and reasons with a partner.

Room	Color	Your reason
a bedroom for a married couple		
a bedroom for a teenaged girl		
a bedroom for a 10-year-old boy		
a kitchen		
a family living room		

GOAL Get to know a new friend

GRAMMAR *Gerunds and infinitives*

Gerunds and infinitives come from verb forms but function as nouns in a sentence, often as direct objects.

Gerund = an -ing form of a verb
She enjoys **painting**.

Infinitive = <u>to</u> + a base form
He wants **to paint** the kitchen yellow.

Use a gerund after the following verbs and expressions: avoid, discuss, dislike, don't mind, enjoy, feel like, practice, quit, suggest

Use an infinitive after the following verbs and expressions: agree, be sure, choose, decide, expect, hope, learn, need, plan, seem, want, wish, would like

Other verbs and expressions can be followed by either a gerund or an infinitive: begin, can't stand, continue, hate, like, love, prefer, start

Remember: There are two other -ing forms:
She is **painting**. (present participle)
The trip was **relaxing**. (participial adjective)

GRAMMAR BOOSTER p. 136
• Gerunds and infinitives: usage within sentences

A **GRAMMAR PRACTICE** Complete the suggestions for ways to make new friends, using the verbs plus gerund or infinitive direct objects.

FIVE WAYS TO MAKE NEW FRIENDS

Everyone .... friends. We .... these principles:

1 want / make   2 suggest / follow

1. .... friendly to everyone you meet. Take advantage of every opportunity.

3 decide / be

2. Even if you .... , ... interest in at least one new person

4 not feel like / socialize   5 learn / show

every day. .... every new acquaintance .... a real friend, but if you

6 not expect   7 become

.... new friends, this is a good way to start.

8 would like / meet

3. .... new acquaintances questions about themselves. People ....

9 be sure / ask   10 enjoy / talk

about themselves.

4. .... too much about yourself. .... people questions about their

11 avoid / talk   12 practice / ask

interests and opinions before you .... them about your own.

13 begin / tell

5. If you .... later, ... something that you both like. If your new friend

14 decide / get together   15 plan / do

has different interests from yours, say you .... something new.

16 not mind / try

B **FIND THE GRAMMAR** Underline all the gerunds and infinitives in the "Answers" section on page 74.

PRONUNCIATION *Reduction of <u>to</u> in infinitives*

▶ 4:03 Notice how an unstressed <u>to</u> reduces to /tə/ in natural speech. Read and listen. Then listen again and repeat.

1 I decided to repaint the bedroom a happier color.

2 We plan to see the World Cup Finals.

3 She doesn't like to hear people talking on cell phones.

4 I know you'd like to choose a more cheerful color.

CONVERSATION MODEL

A ▶4:04 Read and listen to a conversation about likes and dislikes.

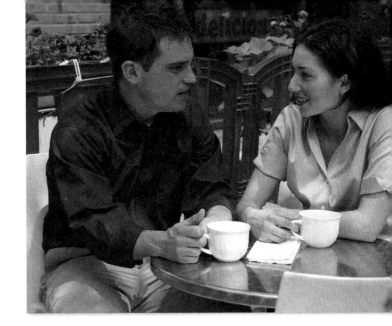

A: So tell me something about yourself.

B: What would you like to know?

A: Well, for example, what do you like doing in your free time?

B: Let's see. Most of all, I enjoy playing tennis. I think it's relaxing. What about you?

A: Well, I find tennis a little boring. But I do love going to the movies.

B: So do I. We should go to the movies together sometime, then.

B ▶4:05 **RHYTHM AND INTONATION** Listen again and repeat. Then practice the Conversation Model with a partner.

NOW YOU CAN   Get to know a new friend

A **NOTEPADDING** List your likes and dislikes in gerund form.

Likes	Dislikes
cooking	skiing

Likes	Dislikes

DIGITAL VIDEO

B **CONVERSATION ACTIVATOR** With a partner, personalize the Conversation Model, using your likes and dislikes in gerund form from your notepad. Change the time or occasion.

A: So tell me something about yourself.
B: What would you like to know?
A: Well, for example, what do you like doing .... ?
B: Let's see. Most of all, I enjoy .... I think it's .... What about you?
A: Well, ...
B: ....

DON'T STOP!
Ask about your partner's plans for this weekend or for a vacation. Use the following verbs and your own infinitives:
  need   want
  plan   would like
For example:
"What do you **plan to do** this weekend?"

Other times and occasions
- in your free time
- on weekends
- on vacations
- with your friends / family
- for lunch / dinner

RECYCLE THIS LANGUAGE.

Positive adjectives	Negative adjectives
awesome	boring
fantastic	awful
wonderful	horrible
great	terrible
terrific	disgusting
relaxing	frightening
interesting	scary
exciting	silly
thrilling	weird
fascinating	

C **CHANGE PARTNERS** Talk about other likes and dislikes.

GOAL Cheer someone up

CONVERSATION MODEL

A ▶4:06 Read and listen to someone trying to cheer a friend up.

A: You look down. What's up?

B: Oh, nothing serious. I'm just tired of the same old grind. But thanks for asking.

A: I know what you mean. I'm tired of working, too. How about going to a movie? That always helps me.

B: Great idea. Let's go this afternoon!

▶4:08 **More adjectives**

down
sad
unhappy
upset
depressed

B ▶4:07 **RHYTHM AND INTONATION** Listen again and repeat. Then practice the Conversation Model with a partner.

GRAMMAR *Gerunds as objects of prepositions*

A gerund can function as an object of a preposition.

	preposition	object
I'm afraid	**of**	**flying**.
She's bored	**with**	**cooking**.
She objects	**to**	**discussing** her feelings.

Be careful! Don't use an infinitive as the object of a preposition.

Don't say: Let's go to a movie instead of ~~to watch~~ TV.

Expressions followed by gerunds

Adjective + preposition

angry about	afraid of
excited about	sick / tired of
depressed about	bored with
happy / sad about	crazy about

Verb + preposition

complain about	apologize for
talk about	believe in
worry about	object to
think about	

With How about or What about
How about [going to a movie]?
What about [leaving work early]?

GRAMMAR BOOSTER p. 136
• Negative gerunds

A **GRAMMAR PRACTICE** Complete the descriptions with prepositions and gerunds.

Ted

Do you want to know what I think?

Ted is an extrovert. Like most extroverts, he's direct. And he's honest; he believes .... the truth to everyone.
1 tell

At his job, he works with other people and he never complains .... long hours. He works hard and doesn't worry .... work on weekends or holidays.
2 work
3 have to

He has a few fears, though. Most of all, he's afraid ....
4 fly

Nicole

I was born in Rome. What about you?

Ted's wife, Nicole, on the other hand, is an introvert. But she doesn't object .... about herself from time to time.
5 talk

Right now, she's bored .... a student, and she's sick and tired
6 be
.... so many long reports and .... exams every few weeks!
7 write
8 take
She's angry .... spend
9 have to
so much time in front of a computer.

However, unlike Ted, she's not at all afraid .... ! She's
10 fly
excited .... on
11 go
vacation.

B **PAIR WORK** Answer the questions about yourself, using gerunds. Then share the information with a partner.

Right now, what are you . . .	
happy about?	
excited about?	
bored with?	
sick and tired of?	

" Right now, I'm happy about getting engaged! "

Cheer someone up

A **NOTEPADDING** Make a list of things that you are tired of. Write them as gerunds.

What are you tired of?
studying so hard

B **CONVERSATION ACTIVATOR** With a partner, role-play cheering someone up. Use your notepad for ideas. Then change roles.

A: You look .... What's up?
B: Oh, nothing serious. I'm just tired of .... But thanks for asking.
A: I know what you mean. ....
B: ....

DON'T STOP!
Make more suggestions, using gerunds and infinitives.

RECYCLE THIS LANGUAGE.

Be sure [to get enough sleep].
You should think about [quitting your job].
What about [going out for a nice dinner]?
How about [getting a massage]?
If you [avoid drinking a lot of coffee], you [will sleep better].
That always helps me.
That's a good idea.
Don't expect [to feel better right away].

C **CHANGE PARTNERS** Cheer your new partner up.

GOAL Discuss personality and its origin

BEFORE YOU READ

EXPLORE YOUR IDEAS In what way does a parent's behavior affect a child's development?

READING ▶ 4:09

Personality: from Nature or Nurture?

What is personality? Many people define personality as a person's usual manner or style of behavior. These patterns of behavior tend to be predictable throughout a person's lifetime. Some people are introverts; others are extroverts. Some people have easygoing personalities: they are usually cheerful and calm and able to cope with life's difficulties without much trouble. Their emotions are usually under control: they don't get extremely angry about little things. Others, at the other end of the personality spectrum, are more emotional, experiencing higher highs and lower lows. Most people's personalities, however, don't fall at the extreme ends but rather fall somewhere in between.

Where do we get our personality? For hundreds of years, psychologists and ordinary people have never stopped debating this fascinating question. Some people think personality develops as a result of the environment—the combination of influences that we learn from, such as our families, our culture, our friends, and our education. The people who believe this theory believe that all babies are born without a personality and that it's the environment that determines, or forms, each child's personality. This school of thought is called the "nurture school."

At the other end of the continuum we find people who believe that personality is determined by "nature," or the characteristics we receive, or "inherit," from our parents biologically, through their genes. These people believe that our personality is not determined by the environment, but rather by genetics, and that each baby is born with a personality.

The "nature-nurture controversy" The nature-nurture controversy is very old. Experimental psychologists have tried to discover which of these two factors, genetics or the environment, is more important in forming our personality. However, it's very difficult, if not impossible, to conduct research on real people with real lives. There's just no way to put people in a laboratory and watch them develop. For this reason, there's no scientific way to settle the nature-nurture controversy. Recently, however, most researchers have come to believe that both the environment AND the genes—nurture and nature—work together and are both important.

Even though the experts have largely discarded the idea that personality development is so black and white, the nature-nurture controversy remains a popular discussion among friends. It seems that everyone has an opinion.

A **UNDERSTAND VOCABULARY FROM CONTEXT** Match the words and phrases in the two columns.

.... **1** genes

.... **2** environment

.... **3** emotions

.... **4** the "nature school" (of thought)

.... **5** the "nurture school" (of thought)

.... **6** personality

a a person's usual pattern of behavior

b what we feel, such as anger, love, and happiness

c the source of traits we inherit from our parents

d the world around us

e the belief that learning determines personality

f the belief that genetics determines personality

B **MAKE PERSONAL COMPARISONS** How is your personality similar to or different from those of your parents? If you have children, how are your children similar to or different from you? Use language from the Reading.

A FRAME YOUR IDEAS Complete the survey to find out if you are an introvert or an extrovert.

ARE YOU AN *EXTROVERT* OR AN *INTROVERT*?

Instructions: From each pair of personality traits, check one that sounds like your personality. At the end, add up your selections for each column. Then decide for yourself: Are you an introvert or an extrovert?

	Extroverts tend to:	Introverts tend to:
1.	○ enjoy being in a group.	○ enjoy being alone.
2.	○ need to interact with others.	○ avoid interacting unnecessarily.
3.	○ be active.	○ be quiet.
4.	○ be interested in events.	○ be interested in feelings.
5.	○ talk without thinking.	○ think without talking.
6.	○ be easy to understand.	○ be hard to understand.
7.	○ know many people a little.	○ know few people, but well.
8.	○ talk.	○ listen.
9.	○ seek excitement.	○ seek peace.
10.	○ express their opinions openly.	○ keep their ideas to themselves.

Total extrovert selections ▭   Total introvert selections ▭

○ **I'm an extrovert.** ○ **I'm an introvert.** ○ **I'm a mixture of both!**

B PAIR WORK Discuss the personality traits you checked. For each, provide a real example from your life to explain your choices.

I'm pretty active. I like to go out almost every night, to the movies or to play sports.

I tend to stay home most nights. It gives me time to think.

C DISCUSSION Where do you think your personality came from, nurture or nature? Did your personality traits come from your parents' genes, or did you <u>learn</u> to be the way you are? Explain with examples using gerunds and infinitives.

RECYCLE THIS LANGUAGE.

[never] complain about __.	be crazy about __.
[sometimes] worry about __.	object to __.
[usually] apologize for __.	believe in __.
get [angry / excited / happy / sad] about __.	not care for __.
	prefer __.
be sick and tired of __.	avoid __.
be bored with __.	not mind __.
be afraid of __.	tend to __.

Text-mining (optional)

Find and underline three words or phrases in the Reading that were new to you. Use them in your Discussion. For example: "easygoing."

GOAL Examine the impact of birth order

BEFORE YOU LISTEN

EXPLORE YOUR IDEAS Do you think the first child in a family has different personality traits from those of siblings who are born later? Explain your answer.

LISTENING COMPREHENSION

A ▶4:10 **LISTEN FOR MAIN IDEAS** Read the statements. Then listen to all three parts of the discussion. Choose the statement that best expresses the main idea of the discussion.

☐ First-born children are often too critical of themselves.

☐ Children in the same family usually have personalities that are determined by order of birth.

☐ Children usually have personalities that are determined by genes.

B ▶4:11 **LISTEN FOR SPECIFIC INFORMATION** Read the exercise. Then listen to each part of the discussion again separately. Complete the exercise as you listen.

Part 1: Check <u>True</u> or <u>False</u> for each statement.

	True	False
1 Brian is usually dissatisfied with himself.	☐	☐
2 Brian obeys rules.	☐	☐
3 Brian does most things well.	☐	☐
4 Brian's mother thinks her husband pushed Brian to be successful.	☐	☐
5 Brian never liked being with adults when he was growing up.	☐	☐

Part 2: Complete each statement by circling the correct information.

1 Annie is (the middle child / the "baby").

2 Annie had (a lot of / only a little) time with her parents before her younger sister was born.

3 Annie is jealous of (Brian / Brian and Lucy).

4 Annie (breaks / obeys) rules.

5 Annie is (rebellious and / rebellious but not) popular.

Part 3: Circle the answer to each question.

1 How old was Annie when Lucy was born?

  a 13 years

  b 13 months

2 What does Lucy like most?

  a making other people laugh

  b laughing at other people

3 What did Lucy do to the dining room wall?

  a She painted it.

  b She washed it.

4 Why does Lucy drive her older siblings crazy?

  a She pays too much attention to them.

  b Others pay too much attention to her.

C **CLASSIFY INFORMATION** Check the most common birth position for each personality, according to the discussion. Listen again if necessary.

Personality traits	First child	Middle child	Youngest child
Breaks rules	☐	☐	☐
Feels less important than siblings	☐	☐	☐
Grows up fast	☐	☐	☐
Grows up slowly	☐	☐	☐
Has a lot of friends	☐	☐	☐
Is creative	☐	☐	☐
Is rebellious	☐	☐	☐
Is self-critical	☐	☐	☐
Plays by the rules	☐	☐	☐
Shows off	☐	☐	☐

NOW YOU CAN Examine the impact of birth order

A **FRAME YOUR IDEAS** Complete the checklist for yourself.

1 **What's your birth position in your family?**
   ○ I'm the first child or the only child in the family.
   ○ I'm a middle child—neither the first nor the last.
   ○ I'm the "baby"—the youngest child in the family.

2 **What are your personality traits?** (Check all that are true.)
   ○ I'm self-critical. I always feel I should do better.
   ○ I'm a rebel.
   ○ I'm popular. I have a lot of friends.
   ○ I feel less important than my older or younger siblings.
   ○ I love to clown around and make people laugh.
   ○ I can be lovable one minute and a rebel the next.
   ○ I'm creative.
   ○ I often feel jealous of my siblings.

B **GROUP WORK** Form three groups of students, according to your birth positions. Compare your checklists with other members of your group. Do you share the same personality traits? Report your findings to the class.

> ❝ Almost everyone in our group checked 'I'm self-critical!' ❞

Group 1: first or only children
Group 2: middle children
Group 3: youngest children

C **DISCUSSION** Talk about how birth order can affect the development of a person's personality.

Ideas
• genetics / nature
• the environment / nurture
• introverts and extroverts
• parents' behavior

REVIEW

A ▶ 4:12 Listen to the conversations. Then circle a word or phrase to complete each statement.

1 Andy is feeling (down / happy).

2 Mollie is (an extrovert / an introvert).

3 Greg is (an extrovert / an introvert).

4 Millie thinks (genetics / the environment) is the most important factor in personality development.

5 Vera thinks (genetics / the environment) is the most important factor in personality development.

B Complete the paragraph with the correct prepositions.

Extroverts don't worry .... talking in public. They believe .... being honest, and they get
         ¹   ²
bored .... being alone. They may talk .... staying home and reading a book, but when they
      ³   ⁴
do, they complain .... having no one to talk to. They object .... being by themselves.
                  ⁵   ⁶

C Complete each personal statement with a gerund or infinitive phrase.

1 When I want to stay healthy, I avoid ....

2 I really enjoy .... on Saturdays and Sundays.

3 I wish other people would quit .... in the movies.

4 Two things I can't stand are .... and ....

5 On weekends, I dislike ....

6 If the weather is bad, I don't mind ....

7 Tomorrow I would really like ....

8 If I want to do well in this class, I need ....

9 Tomorrow I plan ....

10 I think most people are afraid of ....

11 I think people are usually excited about ....

12 Too many people complain about ....

13 My family worries most about ....

D Complete each statement. Circle the best answer.

1 John is such (an extrovert / an introvert). He doesn't like to talk about himself a lot.

2 Our usual pattern of behavior is our (personality / environment).

3 Another word for characteristics is (nurture / traits).

4 Many people believe that (self-criticism / birth order) affects personality development.

5 The nature-nurture controversy is an argument about the origin of the
(environment / personality).

WRITING

Write at least two paragraphs about the personality of someone
you know well. Use vocabulary and ideas from Lessons 3 and 4.

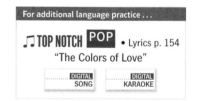

For additional language practice . . .

♫ TOP NOTCH POP • Lyrics p. 154
"The Colors of Love"

| DIGITAL SONG | DIGITAL KARAOKE |

WRITING BOOSTER p. 149
• Parallel structure
• Guidance for this writing exercise

ORAL REVIEW

PAIR WORK

1 Create a conversation for photo 1 in which the girl on the left cheers up her friend. Use gerunds and infinities.

2 Role-play a discussion between the two people in photo 2. They discuss the birth order of their siblings and their personalities.

GROUP WORK Choose one person to be the professor in photo 3. Help that person create a lecture about personality development. Then the other classmates listen to the lecture and ask questions.

You look down . . .

1

So, who is the youngest in your family?

2

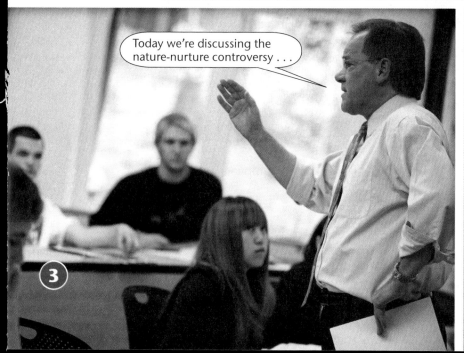

Today we're discussing the nature-nurture controversy . . .

3

✔ NOW I CAN

☐ Get to know a new friend.
☐ Cheer someone up.
☐ Discuss personality and its origin.
☐ Examine the impact of birth order.

COMMUNICATION GOALS

1 Recommend a museum.
2 Ask about and describe objects.
3 Talk about artistic talent.
4 Discuss your favorite artists.

UNIT 8 The Arts

PREVIEW

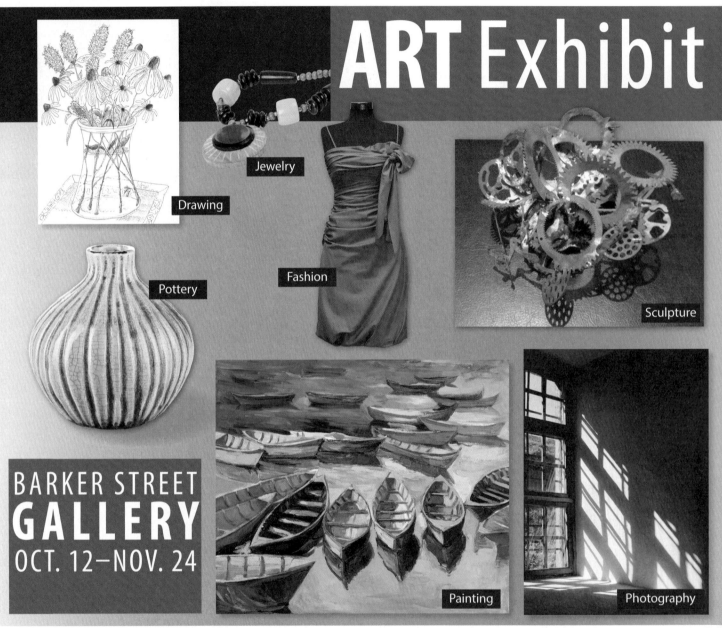

ART Exhibit

Drawing

Jewelry

Fashion

Pottery

Sculpture

Painting

Photography

BARKER STREET GALLERY OCT. 12–NOV. 24

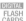 DIGITAL FLASH CARDS

A ▶4:15 **VOCABULARY • *Kinds of art*** Read and listen. Then listen again and repeat.

B **DISCUSSION** What kinds of art do you like? Which pieces of art in the Preview do you like? Why? Use some of the adjectives.

    ❝ I'm not really into paintings, but I think this one's beautiful. ❞

    ❝ I like jewelry, but I don't think the necklace is very interesting. ❞

Adjectives to describe art

beautiful	awful	feminine
exciting	boring	masculine
fascinating	weird	unusual
relaxing	silly	practical
thought-provoking	depressing	interesting

C ▶ 4:16 **PHOTO STORY** Read and listen to a conversation at an art show.

Lynn: Teo, this is just great. I had no idea you had so much talent!

Teo: Thank you!

Lynn: I mean it. Your work is very impressive.

Teo: It's so nice of you to say that. I don't think I'm particularly talented. I just love to paint.

Teo: Believe it or not, these were taken by Paul Johns.

Lynn: Your boss? How do you like that! They're really quite good.

Teo: I know. He doesn't look like the artistic type, does he?

Lynn: No. I had no idea he took photos. I guess you can't always judge a book by its cover.

Teo: Hey, this is an interesting piece. I kind of like it.

Lynn: You do? I find it a little weird, actually.

Teo: But that's what makes it so fascinating.

Lynn: Well, to each his own. I guess I'm just not really into abstract art.

D **ACTIVATE VOCABULARY** Circle the three kinds of art Lynn and Teo discuss:

| painting | fashion | sculpture | photography | drawing | jewelry |

E **FOCUS ON LANGUAGE** With a partner, discuss and find an underlined expression in the Photo Story to match each of the phrases.

1 I didn't know . . .

2 I don't really like . . .

3 Everyone has a different opinion.

4 I have some information that may surprise you.

5 I'm really surprised!

6 You can't really know someone just by looking at him or her.

7 In my opinion, it's . . .

SPEAKING

❝ I prefer more realistic art. I'm just not into abstract paintings. ❞

What kinds of art do you prefer? Explain why.

❝ I'm into fashion. I like clothes that are really modern. ❞

Art can be **realistic** . . .

or **abstract**.

It can be **traditional** . . .

or **modern**.

GOAL Recommend a museum

GRAMMAR *The passive voice*

Most sentences are in the active voice: the subject of a sentence performs the action of the verb. In the passive voice, the receiver of the action is the subject of the sentence.

Active voice: Architect Frank Gehry designed the Guggenheim Museum in Bilbao, Spain.

Passive voice: The Guggenheim Museum in Bilbao, Spain, was designed by architect Frank Gehry.

Form the passive voice with a form of <u>be</u> and the past participle of a verb.

These vases are made in Korea.
The museum was built in the 1990's.
The *Mona Lisa* has been shown at the Louvre Museum since 1797.

It is common to use the passive voice when the performer of the action is not known or not important.
Use a <u>by</u> phrase in a passive voice sentence when it is important to identify the performer of an action.

Pottery is made ~~by people~~ in many parts of the world. (not important)
This bowl was found ~~by someone~~ in Costa Rica. (not important)
This dress was designed by Donatella Versace. (important)

GRAMMAR BOOSTER p. 137
- Transitive and intransitive verbs
- The passive voice: other tenses

A **UNDERSTAND THE GRAMMAR** Read each passive voice sentence and decide if the <u>by</u> phrase is necessary. If it isn't necessary, cross it out.

1 The glass pyramids were added to the Louvre Museum in Paris by workers in 1989.

2 The sculpture *The Thinker* was created by French artist Auguste Rodin.

3 Antoni Gaudí designed and built some of the most famous buildings in Spain. His plans for the Casa Milà in Barcelona were completed by him in 1912.

4 The melody of "Ode to Joy" is known by people all over the world. It was written by German composer Ludwig van Beethoven.

5 China's famous Terracotta Army figures in Xi'an were discovered by farmers in 1974.

B **GRAMMAR PRACTICE** Change each sentence from the active to the passive voice. Use a <u>by</u> phrase.

1 Leonardo da Vinci painted the *Mona Lisa* in the sixteenth century.

....

2 Brazilian photographer Sebastião Salgado took that photograph in 2007.

....

3 Mexican filmmaker Alfonso Cuarón directed the 2013 3D film *Gravity*.

....

4 Japanese master printmaker Katsushika Hokusai made that print over a century ago.

....

5 Korean fashion designer Sang A Im-Propp created these beautiful handbags.

....

6 Weavers have produced beautiful Persian rugs for several thousand years.

....

CONVERSATION MODEL

A ▶4:17 Read and listen to someone recommend a museum.

A: Be sure not to miss the Louvre while you're in Paris.

B: Really? Why's that?

A: Well, for one thing, that famous painting, the *Mona Lisa*, is kept there.

B: No kidding! I've always wanted to see the *Mona Lisa*!

A: Well, they have a great collection of paintings. You'll love it.

B: Thanks for the suggestion!

B ▶4:18 **RHYTHM AND INTONATION** Listen again and repeat.
Then practice the Conversation Model with a partner.

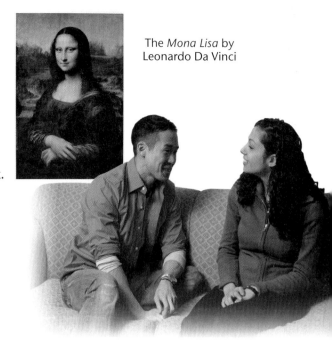

The *Mona Lisa* by
Leonardo Da Vinci

PRONUNCIATION *Emphatic stress*

A ▶4:19 Notice how stress is emphasized to show enthusiasm.
Read and listen. Then listen again and repeat.

1 No KIDDing!   **2** That's fanTAstic!   **3** That's PERfect!   **4** How INteresting!

B Now practice saying the following statements with emphatic stress.

1 That's terRIfic!   **2** That's WONderful!   **3** How exCIting!   **4** How NICE!

NOW YOU CAN Recommend a museum

CONVERSATION ACTIVATOR With a partner, change
the Conversation Model to recommend a museum. Use the
information in the pictures or museums you know. Use the
passive voice and emphatic stress. Then change roles.

A: Be sure not to miss .... while you're in ....
B: Really? Why's that?
A: Well, for one thing, ... is kept there.
B: .... ! I've always wanted to see ....
A: Well, they have a .... collection of .... You'll love it.
B: Thanks for the suggestion!

DON'T STOP!

- Recommend other
  things to see or do.

🔄 RECYCLE THIS LANGUAGE.

Have you ever . . .
- tried __?
- climbed __?
- gone to the top of __?
- gone sightseeing in __?
- taken a tour of __?

THE GOLD MUSEUM - BOGOTÁ

Famous for
its large
collection of
jewelry and
sculpture

El Dorado's Raft
(gold and emeralds)

THE MUSEUM OF MODERN ART
NEW YORK CITY

A fantastic collection of modern
painting, drawing, sculpture, and
photography

Starry Night by Vincent van Gogh

THE NATIONAL
PALACE MUSEUM
TAIPEI

Known for its
huge collection
of traditional
Chinese painting,
pottery, and
sculpture

The Chinese Cabbage
sculpture (jade)

GOAL Ask about and describe objects

CONVERSATION MODEL

A ▶4:20 Read and listen to someone asking about an object.

A: Excuse me. What's this figure made of?
B: Wood. It's handmade.
A: Really? Where was it made?
B: Mexico. What do you think of it?
A: It's fantastic!

B ▶4:21 **RHYTHM AND INTONATION** Listen again and repeat.
Then practice the Conversation Model with a partner.

VOCABULARY *Objects, handicrafts, and materials*

DIGITAL FLASH CARDS

A ▶4:22 Read and listen. Then listen again and repeat.

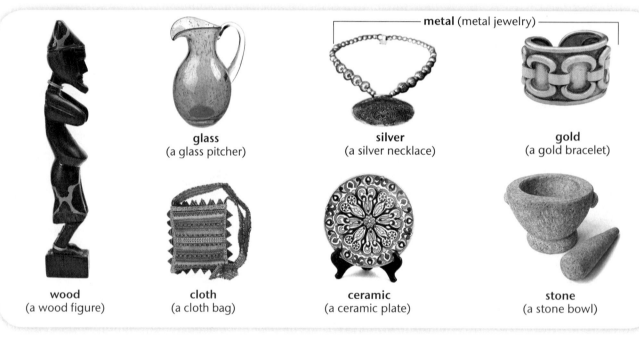

metal (metal jewelry)

glass
(a glass pitcher)

silver
(a silver necklace)

gold
(a gold bracelet)

wood
(a wood figure)

cloth
(a cloth bag)

ceramic
(a ceramic plate)

stone
(a stone bowl)

B **PAIR WORK** Tell your partner about some of your favorite objects in your home.

❝ On my vacation last year, I bought a large stone bowl. It's in my kitchen, and I use it for serving. ❞

GRAMMAR *The passive voice: questions*

Was this stone figure **carved** by hand?	Yes, it was. / No, it wasn't.
Were these wood bracelets **made** in Thailand?	Yes, they were. / No, they weren't.
What **is** this **made** of?	It's made of wood.
What **is** this ceramic bowl **used** for?	It's used for preparing food.
When **was** this picture **painted**?	It was painted in the 1980s.
Where **were** these cloth figures **made**?	In Brazil.
How **were** those handbags **manufactured**?	By machine.

GRAMMAR BOOSTER p. 138
• Yes / no questions in the passive voice: other tenses

A **GRAMMAR PRACTICE** Complete the questions in the interview. Use a question word and the passive voice.

> We interviewed Brian Tardiff at the Sanford Gallery about the exhibit of modern Hmong cloth quilts.
>
> **Q** ...*Where are*... these quilts ...*made*... ?
>   _{1 make}
> **A** These beautiful quilts are made in Vietnam by women from the Hmong tribe.
>
> **Q** .... they .... of?
>   _{2 make}
> **A** They're made of cloth. The pieces of cloth are cut by hand and sewn together.
>
> **Q** .... the cloth .... ?
>   _{3 dye}
> **A** It's dyed in different colors, using plants and beeswax. It takes a lot of time.
>
> **Q** .... they .... ?
>   _{4 sew}
> **A** They are sewn by hand. Each is unique.
>
> **Q** .... they .... for?
>   _{5 use}
> **A** Many people just use them for decoration. However, Hmong culture doesn't have a written tradition, so some are used to tell stories about the women's lives.

B Complete the conversations. Write information questions, using the passive voice.

1 A: .... ?
   B: The glass cups? They were made by hand.

2 A: .... ?
   B: That silver bowl? It's used for serving sugar.

3 A: .... ?
   B: This beautiful figure? It's made of gold.

4 A: .... ?
   B: These wood chairs? They were made in Venezuela.

5 A: .... ?
   B: That Chinese bag? It was made by machine.

6 A: .... ?
   B: This cup? It's made of ceramic.

NOW YOU CAN Ask about and describe objects

A **CONVERSATION ACTIVATOR** With a partner, change the Conversation Model to ask about and describe one of the objects. Use the Vocabulary. Then change roles.

A: Excuse me. What .... made of?
B: ....
A: .... Where .... made?
B: .... What do you think of .... ?
A: ....

DON'T STOP!
• Ask about other objects.
• Ask other passive voice questions.

a figure / Greece

a plate / Italy

a vase / China

dolls / Russia

cups / Thailand

B **CHANGE PARTNERS** Practice the conversation again about other objects.

C **DISCUSSION** Describe an object in your own home. Ask your classmates questions about the objects they describe.

❝ In my living room, I have a small figure. It's made of wood. It's a piece of traditional art. I bought it on my vacation last year. ❞

RECYCLE THIS LANGUAGE.

fantastic	cool
awesome	interesting
terrific	beautiful

BEFORE YOU READ

WARM-UP Do you do anything artistic? Do you paint, draw, or do handicrafts? Why or why not?

> I paint sometimes. I find it relaxing.

> Actually, I'm not interested in art. I don't really think I have any ability.

READING ▶ 4:23

Is it talent or hard work?

When children are asked to draw or paint a picture, they are happy to oblige. And they are willing to talk about and show their creation to anyone they meet. But when adults are asked to do the same thing, they typically get nervous and refuse to even try, claiming that they have no talent.

Most adults see themselves as lacking the "artistic gene." However, when you look at drawings made by artists when they were children, their work doesn't differ much from the scribbles and stick figures all children draw when they are young. When Don Lipski, who makes a successful living as a professional artist, looks back at drawings that he made as a child, he doesn't find any early evidence of his own artistic talent. "I was always making things . . . doodling and putting things together. I didn't think of myself as a creative person. I was just doing what all kids do."

The general belief is that artistic talent is something one is born with: a person either has talent or does not. Clearly, great artists like Michelangelo or Picasso had natural talent and possessed more artistic ability than the average person. However, one factor that isn't often considered is the role that years of training, practice, and

All young children scribble, doodle, and draw stick figures.

hard work have played in the creation of great pieces of art. In addition, most artists are successful because they are passionate about their art—they love what they do. Their passion motivates them to continue to create— and improve their ability—day after day. While natural talent may be an advantage, hard work appears to be a necessary part of the creative process.

In *Drawing on the Right Side of the Brain*, author Betty Edwards argues that while few people are born with natural artistic talent, all of us have the potential to improve our artistic ability. We just have to be willing to keep working at it. She claims that anyone can learn to use the right side of the brain, the side that governs visual skills like drawing and painting. In other words, artistic ability can be learned.

A **RECOGNIZE THE MAIN IDEA** Choose the main idea of the article.

a Artistic skill can be taught.
b Children are better artists than adults.
c To draw well, you have to be born with artistic talent.
d Few people are born with artistic talent.

B **IDENTIFY SUPPORTING DETAILS** Read each statement. Check <u>True</u> or <u>False</u>, according to the article. Support your choice with details from the article.

		True	False
1	Young children generally don't worry if they are talented or not.	☐	☐
2	Most adults think they are not talented.	☐	☐
3	It's easy to see which children are going to be artists when you look at their drawings.	☐	☐
4	There isn't much difference between famous artists and other people.	☐	☐
5	Talent is all one needs to create great artistic work.	☐	☐
6	People who don't have natural talent can improve their artistic skill.	☐	☐

C **PARAPHRASE** Read the paragraph in the article about *Drawing on the Right Side of the Brain* again. In your own words, restate Betty Edwards's theory about artistic ability.

According to Betty Edwards, . . .

NOW YOU CAN Talk about artistic talent

A **FRAME YOUR IDEAS** Complete the survey. Then compare responses with a partner.

Who's Got Talent?

1. Do any of your family members or friends have artistic talent? ○ yes ○ no

   Relationship to you: _____

   In which of the arts? _____

   Where do you think this talent comes from?

   _____

2. Do you think you have natural artistic talent?
   ○ yes ○ no ○ not sure

3. Do other people think you're talented?
   ○ yes ○ no ○ not sure

4. How would you rate your own artistic talent on a scale of 1 to 5?

1	2	3	4	5
POOR		AVERAGE		EXCELLENT

5. In which of the arts do you think you may have talent? Explain.

   example
   ☑ music <u>I sing and play several musical instruments.</u>

   ○ music _____

   ○ drawing / painting _____

   ○ handicrafts _____

   ○ acting _____

   ○ dancing _____

   ○ photography _____

   ○ other _____

B **DISCUSSION** Do you think people are born with artistic talent? Or is it developed through years of training, practice, and hard work?

Text-mining (optional)
Find and underline three words or phrases in the Reading that were new to you. Use them in your Discussion.
For example: "have talent."

GOAL Discuss your favorite artists

BEFORE YOU LISTEN

DIGITAL
FLASH
CARDS

A ▶ 4:24 **VOCABULARY** • *Passive participial phrases* Read and listen.
Then listen again and repeat.

be inspired by   He is inspired by nature. He tries
to capture nature's beauty in his
photographs.

be influenced by She was influenced by Stella
McCartney's work. You can see
similarities between McCartney's
fashion designs and her own.

Stella McCartney
fashion designer

be fascinated by He has always been fascinated by
the life of Vincent van Gogh. He
thinks the artist was extremely
fascinating.

be moved by   You will be moved by Charlie Chaplin's films.
Even though they are funny, their themes of
life and love really touch your heart.

B **PAIR WORK** Tell your partner what inspires, influences, interests,
fascinates, and moves you. Use passive participial phrases.

❝ I'm inspired by my parents. They work really hard. ❞

Vincent van Gogh
painter

Charles Chaplin
actor, filmmaker

LISTENING COMPREHENSION

A ▶ 4:25 **UNDERSTAND FROM CONTEXT** Listen to the interviews.
Complete each statement with the name of the artist.

1 Burt Hildegard is fascinated by the work of ....

2 Susan Wallach is influenced by the work of ....

3 Katherine Wolf is inspired by the work of ....

4 Nick Jenkins is moved by the work of ....

Valentino

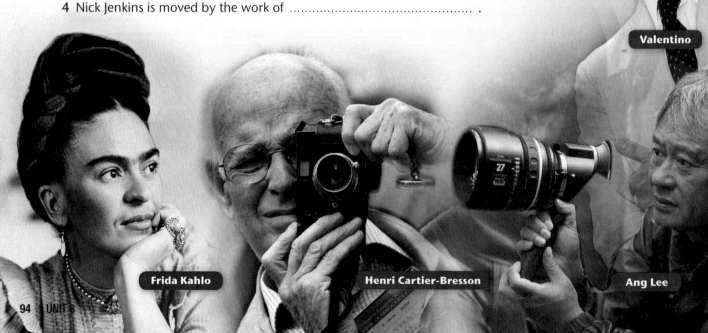

Frida Kahlo   **Henri Cartier-Bresson**   **Ang Lee**

B ▶4:26 **LISTEN TO TAKE NOTES** Listen again to each interview and write some of the details you hear about each artist. Compare notes with a partner.

1 Ang Lee	2 Henri Cartier-Bresson	3 Valentino	4 Frida Kahlo
explores culture	took black-and-white photos	is Italian	was sick as a child

C **DISCUSSION** Which of the artists described in the Listening do you find the most fascinating? Use your notes to explain why.

NOW YOU CAN Discuss your favorite artists

A **FRAME YOUR IDEAS** Complete the questionnaire. Then compare answers with a partner.

WHICH QUALITIES ATTRACT YOU TO AN ARTIST?
Check all that apply.

HIS OR HER WORK . . .

○ is realistic / traditional.
○ is abstract / modern.
○ is easy to understand.
○ makes you think.
○ touches your heart.
○ makes you laugh.
○ other: _____

HE OR SHE . . .

○ is a rebel.
○ is creative.
○ tries new things.
○ has his or her own style.
○ inspires people.
○ other: _____

Types of artists
a painter
a writer
a sculptor
a filmmaker / director
a fashion designer
an architect
a photographer
an actor
a singer
a dancer

Types of art
drawing
painting
sculpture
photography
jewelry
pottery
fashion
handicrafts

B **NOTEPADDING** On your notepad, write about some of your favorite artists.

	Artist's name	Type of artist	Why I like this artist
1			
2			
3			

C **GROUP WORK** Discuss your favorite artists. Tell your class why you like them. Ask your classmates questions about the artists they describe.

I'm a real fan of the Mexican painters Frida Kahlo and Diego Rivera. I'm fascinated by their lives.

Donatella Versace is my favorite designer. Her fashions are so creative!

One of my favorite Japanese artists is Naoki Urasawa. His drawings in the comic book *Yawara!* are really exciting.

A ▶4:27 Listen and write the letter of the piece of art each person is talking about. Then listen again and circle the best way to complete each statement.

a   b   c   d   e

.... **1** She thinks it's (beautiful / ugly / abstract).

.... **2** He thinks it's (traditional / ugly / fascinating). She thinks it's (fantastic / OK / abstract).

.... **3** She thinks it's (OK / awful / great). He thinks it's too (abstract / dark / traditional).

B On a separate sheet of paper, change each sentence from active to passive voice.

1 César Pelli designed the Petronas Twin Towers in Kuala Lumpur.

2 The great Iranian filmmaker Majid Majidi directed *Children of Heaven* in 1998.

3 Henri Matisse made the print *Icarus* in 1947.

4 Annie Leibovitz took that photograph of John Lennon in 1980.

5 The Japanese artist Hokusai produced *The Great Wave of Kanagawa* in the early 1830s.

C List materials under each category. Answers may vary.

Materials that are expensive	Materials that weigh a lot	Materials that break easily
gold		

D Complete the statements.

1 The art of designing clothes is called ....

2 One type of .... is a figure carved from wood or stone.

3 Two types of metal often used to make jewelry are ....
and ....

4 Art in a conservative style from the past is called .... art.

5 A piece of art made with a pen or pencil is called a ....

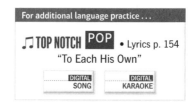

For additional language practice . . .

♫ **TOP NOTCH** **POP** • Lyrics p. 154
"To Each His Own"

DIGITAL SONG   DIGITAL KARAOKE

WRITING

Choose a favorite object that decorates
your home. Describe it in a paragraph.

WRITING BOOSTER p. 150
• Providing supporting details
• Guidance for this writing exercise

Ideas
• a painting or drawing
• a photo or poster
• a piece of furniture
• a figure or sculpture
• a plate, bowl, or vase
• (your own idea) __

ORAL REVIEW

CONTEST Look at the page for one minute and close your books. Using the passive voice, who can describe the most objects and art?

The horse figure is made of __. The statue of David is kept in the __.

PAIR WORK

1 Create a conversation for the man and woman. Recommend a museum. Start like this:

Be sure not to miss the __ while you're in __.

2 Create a conversation for the customer and the store clerk. Ask about the objects. Start like this:

Excuse me. What's this __ made of?

DISCUSSION Talk about the pieces of art in the photos. Say what you like or don't like about each one.

1

THE GREAT MUSEUMS OF EUROPE

The Accademia Gallery
FLORENCE, ITALY

The world's largest collection of statues by Michelangelo!

David by Michelangelo

Musée d'Orsay
PARIS, FRANCE

Home of the best collection of 19th-century French art, including famous painters such as Monet, Degas, and Renoir

Apples and Oranges by Paul Cézanne

2

India

China

Peru

Sweden

✓ NOW I CAN

- ☐ Recommend a museum.
- ☐ Ask about and describe objects.
- ☐ Talk about artistic talent.
- ☐ Discuss my favorite artists.

UNIT 8 97

PREVIEW

COMMUNICATION GOALS

1 Troubleshoot a problem.
2 Compare product features.
3 Describe how you use the Internet.
4 Discuss the impact of the Internet.

Our Community   Friends   Search   Home

FRANK CARUSO

- ✎ Edit
- 🔍 Search
- ✍ Messages
- 📷 My photo albums
- 🎥 Videos
- 👥 Groups
- ⬆ Upload

Frank Caruso Hey, I'm in Rome now! How do you like my new profile pic? That's the Colosseum behind me. This place is awesome!

Kathy Chu Wow! You take good selfies, Frank! You look like you're having fun! Hey, didn't you just post a message from Tokyo two days ago?

Frank Caruso I did. But I've always wanted to see Italy, so someone suggested visiting my airline's web page to look for specials. I got a great deal on a return ticket with a stop here. I'm heading back home to Boston on Friday. Did you all catch the Japan photos I posted?

Nardo Madureira No. What album are they in?

Frank Caruso Actually, they're not here. They're on that new photo-sharing site, GlobalPhoto. Log on and add me to your friends. Or I can send you a link. Click on it to go right to the pics.

Kathy Chu Well, I just looked and they're very cool. Can't wait to see the ones from Italy. I hope they're as nice as the ones from Japan! Nice chatting with you guys! Ciao!

A   **PAIR WORK**   Read the posts on the social network website. Are you on any similar sites? Do you post regularly? Why or why not?

B   **DISCUSSION**   Discuss these questions.

   1 What photo-sharing services do you know about online? Do you store your photos on any of these sites? What are the advantages and disadvantages of photo-sharing services?

   2 Have you ever posted photos while you were traveling? Do you know anyone who has?

C ► 5:02 **PHOTO STORY** Read and listen to a conversation in an office.

Amy: What are you doing here at this hour? I wasn't sure I'd find you.

Dee: Oh hi, Amy. I'm just fooling around online. I guess I forgot about the time!

Amy: Am I interrupting you?

Dee: Not at all. Paul and I are just instant messaging.

Amy: Sorry to bother you. But I'm a little worried about something.

Dee: What's wrong?

Amy: I just got this e-mail from someone I don't know, and I clicked on the attachment to see what it was. My computer totally crashed. Everything froze, and no matter what I do, nothing happens.

Dee: Actually, you should never open an attachment if you don't know the sender. It could be malware or carry a virus.

Amy: I know. I don't know what I was thinking! It just happened so fast.

Dee: Look. First, try shutting down and restarting, OK? Sometimes that takes care of it.

Amy: You think that would work?

Dee: It couldn't hurt. Listen, Paul's still there. Let me send a quick response, OK? I'll just be a second.

Amy: No problem. I'll go and try restarting to see if that does the trick.

D **FOCUS ON LANGUAGE** Look at the five expressions from the Photo Story. Write the letter of the meaning of each expression. (Two expressions have the same meaning.)

.... **1** just fooling around
.... **2** takes care of it
.... **3** couldn't hurt
.... **4** I'll just be a second
.... **5** does the trick

a won't take a long time
b not doing anything serious
c is worth trying
d fixes the problem

SPEAKING

Do you know how to solve computer problems? Complete the chart. Then compare answers with a partner and discuss some possible solutions.

Do you know what to do if . . .	Yes	No	Not sure
1 you think you have a virus?	☐	☐	☐
2 your printer won't print?	☐	☐	☐
3 you click on a link and nothing happens?	☐	☐	☐
4 your computer is really slow?	☐	☐	☐
5 your computer crashes?	☐	☐	☐
6 you forget your password?	☐	☐	☐

Some computer solutions
• try restarting
• check if it's turned on
• buy a new computer
• [your own idea]

GOAL Troubleshoot a problem

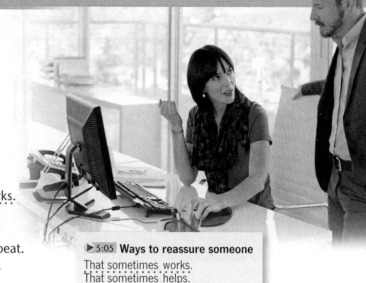

CONVERSATION MODEL

A ▶5:03 Read and listen to people troubleshooting a computer problem.

A: Eugene, could you take a look at this?

B: Sure. What's the problem?

A: Well, I clicked on the toolbar to save a file, and the computer crashed.

B: Why don't you try restarting? That sometimes works.

A: OK. I'll give that a try.

B ▶5:04 **RHYTHM AND INTONATION** Listen again and repeat. Then practice the Conversation Model with a partner.

▶5:05 **Ways to reassure someone**
That sometimes works.
That sometimes helps.
That sometimes does the trick.

VOCABULARY *The computer screen, components, and commands*

DIGITAL FLASH CARDS

A ▶5:06 Read and listen. Then listen again and repeat.

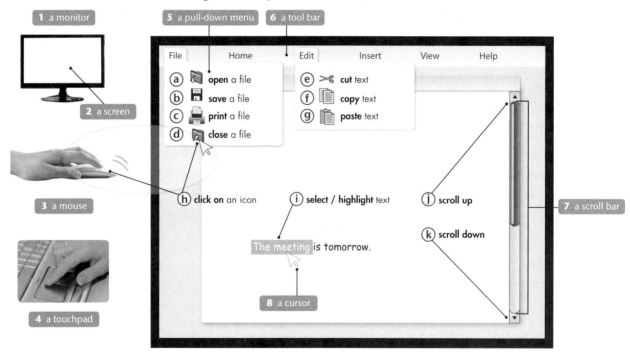

B ▶5:07 **LISTEN TO ACTIVATE VOCABULARY** Listen. Check the computer command each person needs.

	📁	💾	🖨	✂	📄	📋	▲	▼
1 He needs to click on . . .	☐	☐	☐	☐	☐	☐	☐	☐
2 She needs to click on . . .	☐	☐	☐	☐	☐	☐	☐	☐
3 He needs to click on . . .	☐	☐	☐	☐	☐	☐	☐	☐
4 She needs to click on . . .	☐	☐	☐	☐	☐	☐	☐	☐
5 He needs to click on . . .	☐	☐	☐	☐	☐	☐	☐	☐
6 She needs to click on . . .	☐	☐	☐	☐	☐	☐	☐	☐

GRAMMAR *The infinitive of purpose*

GRAMMAR BOOSTER p. 139
- Expressing purpose with <u>in order to</u> and <u>for</u>

An infinitive can be used to express a purpose.

I scrolled down **to read** the text. (= because I wanted to read the text)
Put the cursor on the toolbar **to choose** a file. (= if you want to choose a file)

Answering a <u>Why</u> question with an infinitive of purpose is similar to answering with <u>Because</u>.

Why did you click on that icon?   **To save** the file before I close it. (= Because I want to save it.)
Why did you highlight that word?   **To select** it so I can copy it. (= Because I want to copy it.)

A **FIND THE GRAMMAR** Look at the Conversation Model on page 100. Find an infinitive of purpose. Restate the sentence, using <u>because</u>.

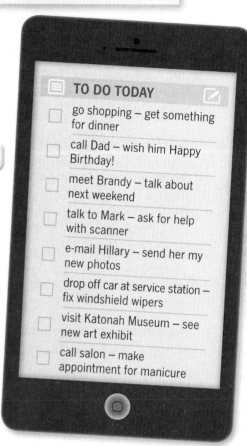

B **PAIR WORK** Look at Cathy's to-do list. Ask and answer questions, using infinitives of purpose.

> 66 Why is Cathy going shopping? 99

> 66 To get something for dinner. 99

TO DO TODAY
- go shopping – get something for dinner
- call Dad – wish him Happy Birthday!
- meet Brandy – talk about next weekend
- talk to Mark – ask for help with scanner
- e-mail Hillary – send her my new photos
- drop off car at service station – fix windshield wipers
- visit Katonah Museum – see new art exhibit
- call salon – make appointment for manicure

C **GRAMMAR PRACTICE** Complete each sentence in your own way. Use infinitives of purpose.

1 Don't forget to click on the save icon *to save your document* .

2 You can click on the print icon ....

3 Put the cursor on the pull-down menu ....

4 I bought a new scanner ....

5 I e-mailed my friend ....

6 I connected to the Internet ....

NOW YOU CAN Troubleshoot a problem

A **CONVERSATION ACTIVATOR** With a partner, change the Conversation Model. Create a conversation in which one of you asks for help with a computer problem. Use the computer vocabulary from page 100 and an infinitive of purpose. Then change roles.

A: .... , could you take a look at this?
B: Sure. .... ?
A: Well, I clicked on .... to .... , and ....
B: Why don't you try .... ? That ....
A: .... I'll give that a try.

DON'T STOP!
- Discuss other problems.
- Offer other suggestions.

RECYCLE THIS LANGUAGE.
- The computer crashes.
- The screen freezes.
- The printer won't print.
- The file won't [open / close / print].
- The [mouse] doesn't work.
- Nothing happens.
- (your own idea) ___

B **CHANGE PARTNERS** Practice the conversation again with other problems.

GOAL Compare product features

GRAMMAR *Comparisons with as . . . as*

To express similarity

Use **as . . . as** with an adjective to indicate how two things are equal or the same. Use the adverb <u>just</u> for emphasis.

The new speakers are **as good as** the old ones.
The iFriend tablet is **just as nice as** the F40.

Use the adverb <u>almost</u> in affirmative statements to indicate that two things are very similar but not exactly the same.

The Zeta B is **almost as fast as** the Panasox.

To express difference

Use <u>not as</u> **. . .** <u>as</u> to indicate how two things are different. Use <u>not quite</u> when the difference is very small. Use <u>not nearly</u> to indicate that there's a big difference.

Our new printer is**n't as noisy as** the old one.
The G4 is**n't quite as expensive as** the Z90.
The Panasox is**n't nearly as affordable as** the Zeta B.

You can use shortened statements with <u>as</u> when the meaning is clear.

The old monitor was great. But the new one is **just as good**. (= just as good as the old one)
Have you seen Carl's new laptop? My laptop isn't **as nice**. (= as nice as his laptop)

> **GRAMMAR BOOSTER** p. 139
> * As . . . as to compare adverbs
> * Comparatives and superlatives: review
> * Comparison with adverbs

A GRAMMAR PRACTICE Read each statement about a product. Write a sentence with <u>as . . . as</u> and the cue to compare the products.

1 The new Shine keyboard is popular. The one from Digitek is popular, too.

(just) ....

2 The XCue joystick is easy to use. The JRock joystick is also easy to use.

(just) ....

3 The C50 monitor is large. The C30 monitor is a little larger than the C50.

(almost) ....

4 Comtec's new mini-tablet is very small. Sango's new mini-tablet is also very small.

(just) ....

5 The CCV speakers are very powerful. The Soundtec speakers are much more powerful.

(not / nearly) ....

6 The Icon monitors are very inexpensive. The Sentinel monitors are a little more expensive.

(not / quite) ....

a joystick

B On a separate sheet of paper, write five statements comparing things you are familiar with. Use <u>as . . . as</u>.

In my opinion, the Mardino sports car isn't nearly as good as the Strega.

> **Ideas for comparisons**
> * cars
> * electronic products
> * stores
> * restaurants
> * (your own idea) ___

DIGITAL
MORE
EXERCISES

PRONUNCIATION *Stress in as . . . as phrases*

A ▶5:08 Read and listen. Then listen again and repeat.

1 The new printer is as slow as the old one.

3 The X12 mouse isn't nearly as nice as the X30.

2 My old smart phone is just as small as the new one.

4 The M200 keyboard isn't quite as cheap as the Z6.

B Read the statements you wrote in Exercise B on page 102 aloud, paying attention to stress.

CONVERSATION MODEL

A ▶5:09 Listen to someone compare product features.

A: I'm thinking about getting a new game controller.

B: Oh, yeah? What kind?

A: Everyone says I should get a Macro.

B: Well, I've heard that the Panatel is as good as the Macro, but it costs a lot less.

A: Really? I'll check it out.

B ▶5:10 **RHYTHM AND INTONATION** Listen again and repeat. Then practice the Conversation Model with a partner.

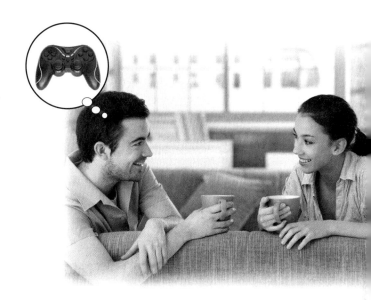

NOW YOU CAN   Compare product features

A **CONVERSATION ACTIVATOR** With a partner, change the Conversation Model, using the magazine ratings to compare features of different products. Use as . . . as. Then change roles.

A: I'm thinking about getting a new ....
B: .... ? What kind?
A: Everyone says I should get ....
B: Well, I've heard that ....
A: Really? ....

DON'T STOP!
• Ask about other features.

RECYCLE THIS LANGUAGE.

Which …
is more popular?
is easier / harder to use?
is lighter / heavier?
is larger / smaller?
is less / more expensive?
costs less / more?

is newer?
is quieter / noisier?
is slower / faster?
has more features?
looks nicer?
gets better reviews?

B **CHANGE PARTNERS** Now practice the conversation again, using other products and features.

Buyer's Friend *Magazine*

Our recommendations!

■ eMax Wireless Mouse	very good	US $25
■ eMax X15 Wireless Keyboard	very comfortable	US $30
■ eMax Y80 Webcam	easy to use	US $52
■ eMax Z40 Monitor	15 inches / 38 centimeters	US $250

THE ELECTRONICS GUIDE

YOUR BEST BUYS!

Klick Wireless Mouse	very good	US $12
Klick P40 Wireless Keyboard	very comfortable	US $25
Klick Ultra Webcam	easy to use	US $52
Klick P20 Monitor	19 inches / 48.3 centimeters	US $99

GOAL Describe how you use the Internet

BEFORE YOU LISTEN

▶ 5:11 **VOCABULARY** • *Internet activities* Read and listen. Then listen again and repeat.

DIGITAL FLASH CARDS

visit a website go to a specific address on the Internet and read its content

surf the Internet visit a lot of different websites for information that interests you

join (an online group) become a member of an Internet group to meet friends and share information about your hobbies and interests

post (a message) add your comments to an online discussion on a message board, a blog, or a social networking site

attach (a file) place a document or photo into an e-mail

upload (a file) move a document, music file, or picture from a personal computer, phone, or MP3 player onto the Internet

share (a link) send an e-mail or post a message with the address of an interesting website you want someone to visit

download an application download a useful program that you can use to play games, get information, or perform tasks

send an instant message "chat" with someone online in real time by typing messages

look up information go to a website to learn about something

> **Remember also:**
> • download (a file)
> • stream a video
> • check e-mail

LISTENING COMPREHENSION

A ▶ 5:12 **LISTEN FOR THE MAIN IDEA** Listen to people describe how they use the Internet. Write a checkmark next to the person who seems to enjoy the Internet the least. Explain your answer.

☐ 1 George Thomas   ☐ 2 Sonia Castro   ☐ 3 Robert Kuan   ☐ 4 Nadia Montasser

B ▶ 5:13 **LISTEN FOR DETAILS** Listen again and check the activities each person does.

	George Thomas	Sonia Castro	Robert Kuan	Nadia Montasser
buys products	☐	☐	☐	☐
downloads music	☐	☐	☐	☐
checks the latest news	☐	☐	☐	☐
participates in online groups	☐	☐	☐	☐
plays online games	☐	☐	☐	☐
sends instant messages	☐	☐	☐	☐
surfs the Internet	☐	☐	☐	☐
uploads photos	☐	☐	☐	☐
uses a computer at work	☐	☐	☐	☐

A   FRAME YOUR IDEAS   Complete the survey about your own Internet use.

New Tab   ×

Internet User Survey

1.   I usually spend ___ hours a week online.

○ 0 – 10   ○ 11 – 20   ○ 21 – 30   ○ 31 – 40   ○ 41 – 50   ○ over 50

2.   I use . . .

○ a desktop   ○ a laptop   ○ a smart phone   ○ a tablet   ○ (none of these)

3.   I use the Internet . . .

○ for work   ○ for study   ○ for fun   ○ I never use the Internet.

4.   I use the Internet . . .

○ to search for new websites	○ to send instant messages	○ to download music
○ to upload photos	○ to keep in touch with friends	○ to upload videos
○ to download photos	○ to keep in touch with family	○ to download videos
○ to design websites	○ to meet new people	○ to send and receive e-mail
○ to look up information	○ to watch movies	○ to play games
○ to create art	○ to look at my bank accounts	○ to pay bills
○ to shop for things	○ to sell things	○ to read or watch the news
○ to take classes	○ to practice English	○ to just fool around
		○ other: ....

5.   Check the statements that are true about you.

○ People consider me to be a technology expert. They come to me for help.
○ You could say I'm an Internet addict. I'm always online.
○ Compared to most people, I spend a lot of time on the Internet.
○ I spend just as much time on the Internet as most people.
○ I don't spend nearly as much time on the Internet as most people.
○ I'm really not comfortable using the Internet.

B   GROUP WORK   Walk around your classroom and ask your classmates about their Internet use. Ask questions to get more information and take notes.

Ideas for questions
Why . . . ?   When . . . ?
Where . . . ?   How . . . ?

Find someone who. . .	Name	Notes
is an Internet expert.		
is an Internet addict.		
isn't comfortable using the Internet.		
uses the Internet to meet people.		
uses the Internet to avoid people.		

C   DISCUSSION   Tell your class what you found out about your classmates and how they use the Internet.

❝ May spends a lot of time online. She uses her tablet to meet new people and keep in touch with friends. Gary spends a lot of time online with his smart phone. He uploads photos and . . . ❞

GOAL Discuss the impact of the Internet

BEFORE YOU READ

1 What kinds of problems have you had on the Internet?

2 What kinds of Internet problems have you heard about on the news?

READING ▶ 5:14

Identity Thieves Steal 40 Million Credit Card Numbers

Eleven hackers around the world were accused of stealing more than 40 million credit card numbers on the Internet. They included three people from the U.S. who are accused of hacking into the wireless networks of popular online stores.

Once inside these networks, they searched for customers' credit card numbers, passwords, and personal information so they could pretend to be those customers. When the identity theft was completed, credit card numbers and other details were then sold on the Internet, allowing criminals to withdraw thousands of dollars at a time from ATMs.

Computer Viruses Are Getting Harder to Prevent

"We're losing the battle against computer viruses," says David Farber, professor of computer science at Carnegie Mellon University. These viruses, which can enter computer systems through junk e-mail from hackers, have reached epidemic proportions, slowing down computers— and sometimes causing whole office computer systems to crash—in both large and small companies. In one year alone, they were reported to have caused $13 billion USD in damage.

Companies have been trying for years to protect themselves with anti-virus programs, but criminals are creating newer, improved viruses faster than these programs can keep up with.

Cyberbullying Leads to Teenager's Death

Megan Taylor Meier, age 13, joined an online social networking group where she became online friends with a 16-year-old boy named Josh. Megan and Josh never communicated by phone or in person, but she enjoyed exchanging messages with him in the group.

Over time, Josh changed. He began to bully her daily—criticizing her personality and telling her what a bad person she was. Some of their communications were posted so everyone could see them. Josh's last message to her said, "The world would be a better place without you." A short time later, Megan committed suicide.

After her death, it was discovered that there was no "Josh." The messages came from the mother of one of Megan's classmates. The mother had been angry with Megan because she believed Megan had said some untrue things about her daughter.

A **UNDERSTAND FROM CONTEXT** Use the context of the articles to help you to complete each definition.

.... **1** A hacker is . . .

.... **2** A computer virus is . . .

.... **3** A criminal is . . .

.... **4** Junk e-mail is . . .

.... **5** An anti-virus program is . . .

.... **6** A cyberbully is . . .

.... **7** An identity thief is . . .

a a software program that causes problems in computers.

b a software program that tries to stop the spread of viruses.

c a person who enters computer systems without permission.

d a person who steals other people's personal information.

e an advertisement you didn't request.

f a person who breaks the law; for example, by stealing money.

g a person who sends cruel and negative messages to another person online.

B **RELATE TO PERSONAL EXPERIENCE** What news stories have you heard about the Internet? Do you ever worry about using the Internet? Why or why not?

A **NOTEPADDING** With a partner, discuss each statement. Write at least one good change and one bad change for each.

1	The Internet has changed the way people find information.
	Good changes:
	Bad changes:

2	The Internet has changed the way people work in offices.
	Good changes:
	Bad changes:

3	The Internet has changed the way people shop.
	Good changes:
	Bad changes:

4	The Internet has changed the way people communicate.
	Good changes:
	Bad changes:

B **DISCUSSION** Do you think that computers and the Internet have brought more benefits or more problems? Support your opinions with examples.

Text-mining (optional)
Find and underline three words or phrases in the Reading that were new to you. Use them in your Discussion.
For example: "exchanging messages."

In my opinion, there are more benefits than problems. For example, it's easy to look up information, and it's really fast.

I think the Internet is OK, but there are really too many problems. First of all, you have to be very careful if you shop online with a credit card.

REVIEW

A ▶5:15 Listen to the conversations. Circle T for true and F for false. Then listen again and infer how to complete each statement.

1	She recommends the C40.	T	F
2	She recommends the Hip web camera.	T	F
3	He recommends the new Sender tablet.	T	F
4	He recommends the Play Zone 3.	T	F

1 The C40's monitor is .... the X8's.
  a the same size as   **b** larger than   **c** smaller than

2 The Hip web camera is .... the Pentac web camera.
  a the same price as   **b** cheaper than   **c** more expensive than

3 Sender's new model is .... Sender's old model.
  a the same as   **b** nicer than   **c** worse than

4 Play Zone 3 is .... Play Zone 2.
  a as cool as   **b** less cool than   **c** more cool than

B Answer each question in your own words, using infinitives of purpose.

1 Why do people join social networking sites? ....

2 Why do people send instant messages? ....

3 Why do people surf the Internet? ....

4 Why do people shop online? ....

5 Why are you studying English? ....

C Complete each statement.

1 .... on an icon on the screen to select it.

2 If you want to print a document, click on the print icon on the ....

3 To read more text on your monitor's .... , use the scroll .... to scroll down.

4 Click on <u>File</u> on the toolbar so you can choose an icon from the .... menu.

5 When you're finished working on a document, don't forget to .... it before you close the file.

D Unscramble the letters of the words in the box to complete each sentence.

chatated	clorls	doalwond	esmou	rekcha	rusvi

1 Last year, a .... got into the company's computer systems and stole important information.

2 Use the .... to click on a file and open it.

3 It isn't difficult to .... songs from the Internet.

4 Use the .... bar to see more text on the screen.

5 Her computer isn't working now because she downloaded a .... from a piece of junk e-mail.

6 I .... the photos to the e-mail I sent this morning.

WRITING

Write two paragraphs about the benefits and the problems of the Internet. Use your notepads from page 107 for support.

For additional language practice . . .

♫ TOP NOTCH **POP** • Lyrics p. 154
"Life in Cyberspace"

| DIGITAL SONG | DIGITAL KARAOKE |

WRITING BOOSTER p. 151
• Organizing ideas
• Guidance for this writing exercise

ORAL REVIEW

CONTEST Look at the photos for one minute. Then close your books. Who can name all the computer parts and activities in the photos? For example:

There's a printer and . . . OR
He's trying to print photos . . .

PAIR WORK

1 Create a conversation for the man and the woman. They are troubleshooting a problem. Start like this:
Could you take a look at this?

2 Create a conversation for the two men. One is asking for a product recommendation. Start like this:
I'm thinking about getting a new . . .

3 Create a conversation for the two women on the phone. One is asking the other about what she is doing on the computer. Start like this:
Am I interrupting you?

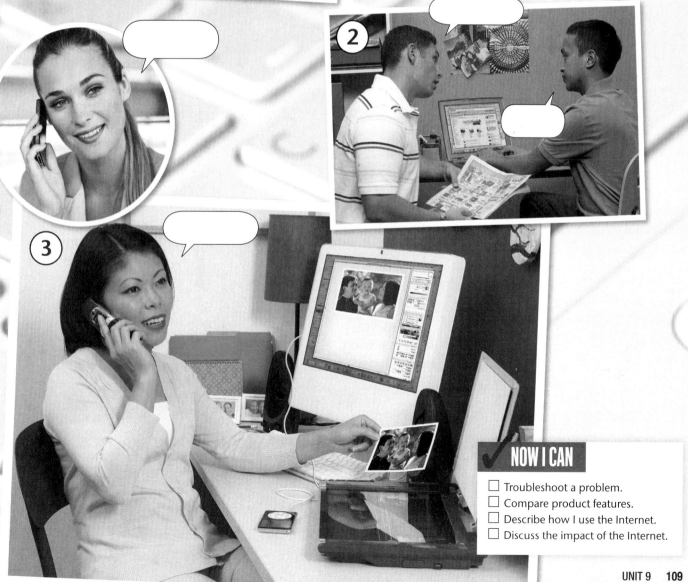

NOW I CAN

☐ Troubleshoot a problem.
☐ Compare product features.
☐ Describe how I use the Internet.
☐ Discuss the impact of the Internet.

UNIT 10 Ethics and Values

PREVIEW

MORAL DILEMMAS
What should they do?

This box has the wrong price.

Uh-oh. Someone forgot that watch.

Andrew

Victoria

Amber

Daniel

I think this total is wrong.

But I only ordered one!

Guest Check

			CHECK NO. 2651	
1	shrimp cocktail		9	50
1	tomato bisque		4	50
1	garden salad		6	75
1	sirloin		18	95
1	bottle sparkling water		3	00
1	espresso		2	50
	TOTAL		22	20

Thank You - Call Again

GUEST RECEIPT
CHECK NO. 2651

AJ's OUTDOOR GEAR   INVOICE

DESCRIPTION	QUANTITY	UNIT PRICE
Nylon windbreaker	1	$52.99
	TOTAL	$52.99

A GROUP WORK Have you ever been faced with a moral dilemma similar to the ones in the pictures? Tell your classmates what happened.

B ▶5:18 **PHOTO STORY** Read and listen to a conversation about a moral dilemma.

Matt: I can't believe it! I just picked this up to look at it and the thing broke in two. And with these ridiculous prices, it's going to cost me an arm and a leg.

Noah: Oh, forget it. I'll bet it was already broken.

Matt: You're probably right.

Noah: Just put it back on the shelf. The place is empty. No one saw. Let's just split.

Matt: I couldn't do that.

Noah: Why not? You said it yourself. The prices are ridiculous.

Matt: Well, put yourself in the owner's shoes. Suppose the plate were yours? How would you feel if someone broke it and didn't tell you?

Noah: Well I'm *not* the owner. And, anyway, for him it would be just a drop in the bucket. To *you* it's a lot of money.

Matt: Maybe so. But if I ran out without telling him, I couldn't face myself.

C **FOCUS ON LANGUAGE** Match each idiom from the Photo Story with its meaning.

1 an arm and a leg
2 split
3 put yourself in someone's shoes
4 a drop in the bucket
5 I couldn't face myself.

a a small amount of money
b I would feel bad about it.
c a lot of money
d imagine another person's point of view
e leave

D **THINK AND EXPLAIN** Answer the following questions. Support your answers with quotations from the Photo Story.

1 Does Noah think Matt broke the plate?
2 Why does Noah think it would be easy to leave without saying anything?
3 What does Matt want to do about the plate?

SPEAKING

A **SURVEY** Look at "Moral Dilemmas" and the Photo Story again. Do you agree with the statements below? Circle <u>yes</u> or <u>no</u>, and then give a reason for your answers.

1 Andrew should buy the chocolate with the lower price.	yes / no	
2 Victoria should keep the watch.	yes / no	
3 Amber should tell the waiter there's a mistake.	yes / no	
4 Daniel should send the second jacket back.	yes / no	
5 Matt should tell the store owner what happened.	yes / no	

B **GROUP WORK** Form small groups. Compare your answers and explain your reasons.

GOAL Discuss ethical choices

GRAMMAR *The unreal conditional*

Remember: Conditional sentences express the results of actions or conditions. The real conditional expresses the results of real conditions—conditions that exist.
If I don't use English in class, I won't learn to speak it.

Meaning

Unreal conditional sentences describe the results of unreal conditions—conditions that don't exist.

unreal action or condition	result (if it were true)
If I **found** a wallet in the street,	I**'d try** to return it. (unreal: I haven't found one.)

Contraction
would → 'd

Formation

In the <u>if</u> clause, use the simple past tense. For the verb <u>be</u>, always use <u>were</u>.
In the result clause, use <u>would</u> + a base form.

unreal action or condition	result (if it were true)
If I **had** to make a hard decision,	I **would try** to do the right thing
If she **knew** how to speak French,	she**'d help** them.
If you **broke** something in a store,	**would** you **pay** for it?
If you **were** Matt,	what **would** you **do**?
If I **were** you,	I **wouldn't do** that.
If you **weren't** my friend,	I **wouldn't tell** you what happened.

Be careful!

Don't use <u>would</u> in the <u>if</u> clause.
If I knew his name, I would tell you.
NOT   If I ~~would know~~ his name . . .

Note: In real and unreal conditional sentences, the clauses can occur in either order. Use a comma if the <u>if</u> clause comes first.

If I knew, I would tell you. OR I would tell you **if I knew.**

GRAMMAR BOOSTER p. 140

Expressing ethics and obligation: expansion
• <u>should</u>, <u>ought to</u>, <u>had better</u>
• <u>have to</u>, <u>must</u>, <u>be supposed to</u>

A **UNDERSTAND THE GRAMMAR** Check the conditional sentences that describe an unreal condition.

☐ **1** If we ate in a restaurant, I would pay the bill.

☐ **2** I'll pay the bill if we eat in a restaurant.

☐ **3** If you get a haircut, you'll look younger.

☐ **4** His wife would worry if he came home really late.

☐ **5** If I were you, I'd tell him the truth.

☐ **6** If I have problem with my office computer, I always ask my co-worker Jim to help.

☐ **7** If they sent me the wrong pants, I would return them.

B **GRAMMAR PRACTICE** Complete each unreal conditional sentence with the correct forms of the verbs.

1 If they .... the wrong price on the coat, ... you .... it without telling
         put   buy
    the clerk?

2 I'm sure you .... something if the restaurant check .... wrong.
                say   be

3 If I .... an expensive piece of jewelry in a public bathroom and .... find the owner,
         find   can not
    I .... it.
     not keep

4 If you .... friends with someone who did something wrong, ... you ....
         be   say
    something to him or her?

5 If you .... two tickets, ... you .... one to a friend?
         have   give

6 What .... if it .... here tomorrow?
        happen   snow

7 They .... to India if they .... the money.
        go   have

8 If you .... two jackets instead of the one you ordered, ... you .... one
        receive   send
    of them back?

9 If they .... here, I .... them what happened.
        be   tell

CONVERSATION MODEL

A ▶5:19 Read and listen to people discussing an ethical choice.

A: Look at this. They didn't charge us for the desserts.

B: Really? I think we'd better tell the waiter.

A: You think so?

B: Absolutely. If we didn't tell him, it would be wrong.

B ▶5:20 **RHYTHM AND INTONATION** Listen again and repeat. Then practice the Conversation Model with a partner.

▶5:21 **Express an ethical obligation**

We'd better tell	
We should tell	the waiter.
We ought to tell	

PRONUNCIATION *Blending of d + y in would you*

A ▶5:22 Notice how the /d/ and /y/ sounds blend to /dʒ/ in questions with "would you." Read and listen. Then listen again and repeat.

1 What would you do if the waiter didn't charge you for the dessert?

2 What would you do if you found a wallet on the street?

3 Who would you call if you were sick?

4 Where would you go if you wanted a great meal?

B **PAIR WORK** Complete the following questions. Ask a partner the questions, using blending with would you. Then answer your partner's questions.

1 What would you do if .... ?

2 Where would you go if .... ?

3 When would you eat if .... ?

NOW YOU CAN Discuss ethical choices

A **CONVERSATION ACTIVATOR** With a partner, change the Conversation Model. Discuss ethical choices, using the situations in the pictures. Then change roles.

A: Look .... They ....
B: .... ? I think .... 'd better ....
A: You think so?
B: Absolutely. If .... , ...

DON'T STOP!
• Say more.

🔄 **RECYCLE THIS LANGUAGE.**
I couldn't face myself.
Put yourself in [his / her / their] shoes.
If you don't tell the [clerk], [she'll have to pay for it].
If [he didn't charge us], [we would tell him].

▶5:23 **Situations that require an ethical choice**

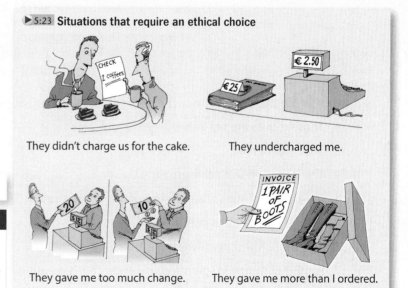

They didn't charge us for the cake.

They undercharged me.

They gave me too much change.

They gave me more than I ordered.

B **DISCUSSION** Tell your classmates about an ethical choice you had to make in the past.

CONVERSATION MODEL

A ▶5:24 Read and listen to a conversation about returning property.

A: Excuse me. I think you forgot something.

B: I did?

A: Isn't this jacket hers?

B: Oh, you're right. It is. That's nice of you.

A: Don't mention it.

> ▶5:26 **Acknowledging thanks**
> Don't mention it.
> My pleasure.
> You're welcome.
> Not at all.

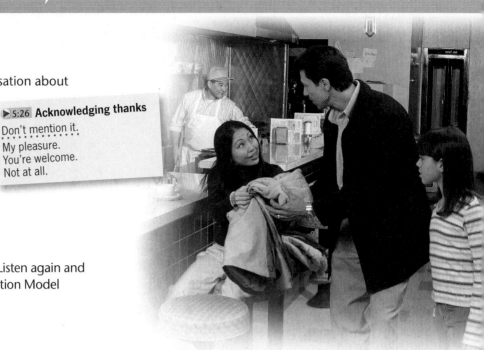

B ▶5:25 **RHYTHM AND INTONATION** Listen again and repeat. Then practice the Conversation Model with a partner.

GRAMMAR *Possessive pronouns / Whose*

Possessive pronouns can replace nouns and noun phrases. They answer questions with Whose and clarify answers to questions with Which.

A: **Whose** coat is that? B: It's **mine**. (= It's my coat.)
A: **Which** is her cup? B: This one is **hers**.

subject pronouns	possessive adjectives	possessive pronouns	
I	my	mine	That's my jacket. / It's mine.
you	your	yours	Your dinner was great. / Yours was great.
he	his	his	Are these his keys? / Are these his?
she	her	hers	She drives her car to work. / She drives hers to work.
we	our	ours	These are our shoes. / These are ours.
they	their	theirs	They finished their assignment. / They finished theirs.

> **Be careful!**
> • Don't use a possessive adjective in place of a possessive pronoun.
>   Is this **yours**? NOT Is this ~~your~~?
> • Don't use a noun after a possessive pronoun.
>   These shoes are **mine**. NOT These are ~~mine shoes~~.

> **GRAMMAR BOOSTER** p. 141
> • Possessive nouns: review and expansion
> • Pronouns: summary

A GRAMMAR PRACTICE Replace the noun phrases with possessive pronouns.

1 Those gloves are ~~my gloves~~. *mine*

2 That is ~~her coat~~.

3 The books on that table are ~~Mr. Davison's~~.

4 Their car and ~~our car~~ are parked on the same street.

5 Are those my tickets or ~~her tickets~~?

6 The white house is ~~my mother's house~~.

7 Is this painting ~~your painting~~ or ~~her brother's painting~~?

8 The newspaper under the chair is ~~his daughter's paper~~.

9 Is this DVD ~~your DVD~~ or ~~your friends'~~?

10 Are these ~~your son's shoes~~?

B **GRAMMAR PRACTICE** Complete the conversations. Circle the correct adjectives and pronouns.

1 A: Whose umbrella is this, (he / his) or (her / hers)?
   B: I'm not sure. Ask them if it's (their / theirs).

2 A: Who is more conservative about clothes? Your parents or your husband's parents?
   B: (He / His), I think. (My / Mine) parents are pretty liberal.

3 A: Is this (ours / our) suitcase?
   B: No, I already got (our / ours) suitcase, so this one can't be (our / ours).

4 A: I found this necklace near Carrie's desk. Is it (her / hers)?
   B: No, it's (my / mine) necklace. I'm so happy someone found it!

5 A: Is that (their / theirs) car?
   B: No, (their / theirs) is the black one over there.

6 A: Where should we meet? At (your / yours) house or (my / mine)?
   B: Neither. Let's meet at (my / mine) office.

C ▶5:27 **LISTEN TO ACTIVATE GRAMMAR** Listen to the conversations and complete each statement with a possessive pronoun.

1 The bag is ....
2 The phone is .... , but the keys belong to Brad's wife. They're ....
3 The coat isn't ....
4 The concert tickets aren't ....

NOW YOU CAN Return someone else's property

A **CONVERSATION ACTIVATOR** With a partner, change the Conversation Model to role-play returning the items in the pictures. Then change roles.

A: Excuse me. I think you forgot something.
B: I did?
A: .... yours?
B: Oh, you're right. .... That's nice of you.
A: ....

B **GROUP WORK** First, collect personal items from your classmates. Then role-play returning someone else's property. Walk around the room to find the owners. Use possessive pronouns.

C **EXTENSION** Place all your classmates' personal items on a table. Ask about each item. Identify the owner, using possessive pronouns.

❝ Whose phone is this? ❞

❝ It's his. ❞

GOAL Express personal values

BEFORE YOU LISTEN

EXPLORE YOUR IDEAS Which actions would be OK, and which wouldn't be OK for the following people: you? your parents? your grandparents? your own teenaged child?

> 66 It wouldn't be OK if my grandmother pierced her nose. Face piercing is for young people. She's too old. 99

get a tattoo

pierce one's ears, face, or body

dye one's hair a wild color

LISTENING COMPREHENSION

A ▶ 5:28 **LISTEN FOR MAIN IDEAS** Listen to each conversation. Then circle the correct word or phrase to complete each statement.

1 a Beth thinks it's (OK / not OK) to wear an earring to the office.

   b Beth (convinces / doesn't convince) Luke.

2 a Celia's husband thinks it's (OK / wrong) for a woman to have a tattoo.

   b Celia's husband thinks it's (OK / wrong) for a man to have a tattoo.

3 a The first man is (happy / not happy) that his daughter is going to law school.

   b He wants his daughter to (stay home / work).

4 a Kate's dad is (worried / not worried) about what people think of Kate.

   b Kate is (worried / not worried) about what people think of her.

B **UNDERSTAND VOCABULARY FROM CONTEXT** Read the following quotations from the conversations. Then choose the meaning of each underlined word or phrase. Listen again if necessary.

1 "But lots of people are <u>old-fashioned</u>, and they don't think men should wear earrings."

   a preferring the way things were in the past

   b preferring the way things are now

2 "What a <u>double standard</u>!"

   a having the same rules for everyone

   b having different rules for different people

3 "That's a little <u>sexist</u>, if you ask me!"

   a not treating men and women in the same way

   b treating men and women in the same way

4 "But <u>modesty</u> is very important for girls."

   a wearing clothes that cover one's body

   b wearing clothes that show one's body

C **APPLY NEW VOCABULARY** Write an example for each word or phrase from your own experience. Compare examples with a partner.

> 66 I think an example of old-fashioned is not letting teenagers go out on dates. 99

old-fashioned	
a double standard	
sexist	
modesty	

D **PAIR WORK** Discuss the picture. Use the following words and phrases in your discussion: old-fashioned, sexist, double standard, modesty.

> 66 He's measuring the woman's swimsuit. If she were a man, he wouldn't measure it. That's a double standard. 99

Man measuring the length of a woman's swimsuit (U.S., 1920s)

NOW YOU CAN Express personal values

A **IDEA FRAMING** Complete the Values Self-Test. Then compare answers with a partner. Do you have the same values?

Values Self-Test

Check the boxes that best describe your values. Include a specific example.

1. ❏ I'm modern in my attitudes about modesty.
   ❏ I'm old-fashioned in my attitudes about modesty.
   Explain. _____
   _____
   _____

2. ❏ I think tattoos and body piercing are OK for men.
   ❏ I think tattoos and body piercing are OK for women.
   Explain. _____
   _____
   _____

3. ❏ I think it's OK to have a double standard for different people.
   ❏ I think the rules should be the same for everyone.
   Explain. _____
   _____
   _____

4. ❏ Some people might say I'm sexist.
   ❏ Nobody would say I'm sexist.
   Explain. _____
   _____
   _____

B **NOTEPADDING** Answer each question and explain your opinion, using examples.

Is it sometimes OK to have a double standard for men and women?

Can people be sexist when they talk about men, or only about women?

Are old-fashioned ideas usually better or worse than modern ideas?

C **GROUP WORK** Now discuss each question, expressing your personal values. Expect people to disagree with you!

> ↻ **RECYCLE THIS LANGUAGE.**
>
> | Agreement and disagreement | Likes and dislikes | Adjectives |
> |---|---|---|
> | I agree. | I like __. | liberal |
> | I disagree. | I dislike __. | conservative |
> | It depends. | I hate __. | strict |
> | | I can't stand __. | modest |
> | | I don't mind __. | |
> | | __ drives me crazy! | |

GOAL Discuss acts of kindness and honesty

BEFORE YOU READ

PREDICT Look at the headlines of the three news stories. In what way do you think the stories will be similar?

READING ▶ 5:29

Homeless Man Returns Wallet with $900

Posted on: Monday, 17 April

SANTA ANA, Calif. - A homeless man searching through trash bins for recyclable cans found a missing wallet and returned it to its owner. Kim Bogue, who works in the city, realized that her wallet was missing last week and doubted she'd ever get back the $900 and credit cards inside. "I prayed that night and asked God to help me," said Bogue, who was saving the money for a trip to her native Thailand.

Days later, a homeless man found the wallet wrapped in a plastic bag in the trash, where Bogue had accidentally thrown it away with her lunch. He gave it to Sherry Wesley, who works in a nearby building. "He came to me with the wad of money and said, 'This probably belongs to someone that you work with. Can you return it?'" Wesley said.

"He has a very good heart," said Bogue, who gave the man a $100 reward. "If someone else had found it, the money would have been gone."

Man Risks Life to Save Another

Many people who ride a busy urban subway wonder, "What would happen if I fell off the platform and onto the tracks? What would I do?" Others wonder, "What would I do if someone else fell?"

That question was answered in a split-second decision made by "subway hero" Wesley Autrey, a fifty-year-old New York City construction worker on his way to work. Autrey jumped onto the tracks to save a fellow passenger from an oncoming New York City subway train.

The passenger, Cameron Hollopeter, 20, a film student at the New York Film Academy, had fallen between the tracks after suffering a seizure. Autrey rolled Hollopeter into a gap between the rails and covered him with his own body just as the train entered the station. Both men survived.

"I don't feel like I did something spectacular; I just saw someone who needed help," Mr. Autrey said. "I did what I felt was right."

An act of honesty by airport screener

NEW DELHI: In a display of honesty, a security agent at the Indira Gandhi International Airport handed over a small plastic bag with US $3,000 in cash to a passenger who had completely forgotten the bag after it passed through the airport screening machine.

Noticing that the bag had been left behind, Dalbir Singh made an announcement asking passengers to come forward to claim it. However, when no one claimed it, Singh inspected the baggage tag and guessed it probably belonged to a passenger en route to Mumbai. An announcement was made on the next flight to Mumbai, and the owner of the bag came forward to collect it.

Singh was given a cash reward for his honesty.

A **SUMMARIZE** Summarize one of the articles. Close your book and tell the story in your own words.

B **INTERPRET INFORMATION** Discuss each person's motives for his or her actions.

1 Why did Kim Bogue give the homeless man a reward?

2 Why did Wesley Autrey risk his life to save a stranger?

3 Why do you think Dalbir Singh returned the money to the passenger?

C **RELATE TO PERSONAL EXPERIENCE** Think of a story you have heard about someone who helped a stranger in need. Tell it to the class.

A **NOTEPADDING** Answer the questions about each situation.

Situation: Someone ahead of you at a coffee bar has paid for your coffee.

What could you do?

What should you do?

What would you do?

What would most people do?

Situation: A blind man is crossing a street in front of you and a car is coming.

What could you do?

What should you do?

What would you do?

What would most people do?

Situation: You find a wallet full of cash in a restaurant.

What could you do?

What should you do?

What would you do?

What would most people do?

Situation: You find cash at an ATM.

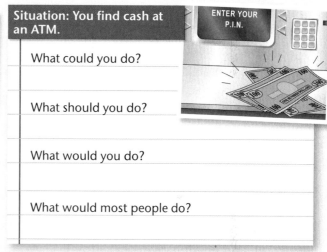

What could you do?

What should you do?

What would you do?

What would most people do?

Situation: The cashier undercharges you.

What could you do?

What should you do?

What would you do?

What would most people do?

Situation: You find a gold watch in a department store dressing room.

What could you do?

What should you do?

What would you do?

What would most people do?

B **GROUP WORK** Compare your notes. Would you all do the same things in these situations? Use the unreal conditional and expressions from the Photo Story on page 111.

> 66 If I found cash near an ATM, I would keep it. There would be no way to find the owner. 77

Text-mining (optional)
Find and underline three words or phrases in the Reading that were new to you. Use them in your Group Work
For example: "a split-second decision."

REVIEW

A ▶ 5:30 Listen to the conversations. Check <u>Yes</u> or <u>No</u> to answer each question and explain your answers.

		Yes	No
1	Do you think John has a double standard?	☐	☐

Explain your answer: ....

2 Do you think Jessica's mom is sexist? ☐ ☐

Explain your answer: ....

3 Do you think Alex's dad is old-fashioned? ☐ ☐

Explain your answer: ....

B Complete the questions with <u>Whose</u>. Then answer each question, using possessive pronouns. Follow the example.

1 Those shoes belong to my daughter. ....*Whose are*.......... they? ...*They're hers.*..........

2 That sweater belongs to my son. .... it? ....

3 The house across the street is my parents' house. .... it? ....

4 These tickets are my husband's and mine. .... they? ....

5 The table over there is your table. .... it? ....

C Complete each conditional sentence in your own words.

1 If the weather were good, ...

2 If .... , I'd go out to eat tonight.

3 If I found your wallet, ...

4 If .... , I'd call home.

5 I'd be angry with my children if ....

6 If I had a new car, ...

7 I would choose a new career if ....

> **For additional language practice . . .**
>
> ♫ TOP NOTCH **POP** • Lyrics p. 154
> "What Would You Do?"
>
> DIGITAL SONG   DIGITAL KARAOKE

D What would you do? Complete each unreal conditional sentence.

1 You order two sandwiches for lunch, but they only charge you for one.

YOU "If the restaurant undercharged me, I ...."

2 You pay for a newspaper that costs one dollar with a five-dollar bill. The merchant gives you nine dollars change.

YOU "If the merchant gave me too much change, I ...."

3 You buy a smart phone from a website. When the package arrives, you see that the company has sent you two MP3 players and the smart phone.

YOU "If the company sent me more items than I paid for, I ...."

WRITING

Write three paragraphs about Matt's dilemma in the Photo Story on page 111. In the first paragraph, summarize the situation. In the second paragraph, write about what Matt could or should do. In the third paragraph, write what you would do if you were Matt. Explain your reasons, using the unreal conditional.

> **WRITING BOOSTER** p. 152
> • Introducing conflicting ideas
> • Guidance for this writing exercise

ORAL REVIEW

CONTEST Form teams. With your team, look at the two pictures for one minute. Then close your books and tell the story you saw in the pictures. The team that remembers more details wins.

PAIR WORK

1 Tell your partner what you would do if you were the woman who found the lost object. Use the unreal conditional. Start like this:

If I found ..., I would ...

2 Create a conversation for the people in the second picture. Use possessive pronouns. Start like this:

Excuse me. Is this your ...

NOW I CAN

- ☐ Discuss ethical choices.
- ☐ Return someone else's property.
- ☐ Express personal values.
- ☐ Discuss acts of kindness and honesty.

Reference Charts

PRONUNCIATION TABLE

Vowels

Symbol	Key Words
i	beat, feed
ɪ	bit, did
eɪ	date, paid
ɛ	bet, bed
æ	bat, bad
ɑ	box, odd, father
ɔ	bought, dog
oʊ	boat, road
ʊ	book, good
u	boot, food, flu
ʌ	but, mud, mother
ə	banana, among
ɚ	shirt, murder
aɪ	bite, cry, buy, eye
aʊ	about, how
ɔɪ	voice, boy
ɪr	deer
ɛr	bare
ɑr	bar
ɔr	door
ʊr	tour

Consonants

Symbol	Key Words	Symbol	Key Words
p	pack, happy	z	zip, please, goes
b	back, rubber	ʃ	ship, machine, station, special, discussion
t	tie		
d	die	ʒ	measure, vision
k	came, key, quick	h	hot, who
g	game, guest	m	men
tʃ	church, nature, watch	n	sun, know, pneumonia
dʒ	judge, general, major	ŋ	sung, ringing
f	fan, photograph	w	wet, white
v	van	l	light, long
θ	thing, breath	r	right, wrong
ð	then, breathe	y	yes
s	sip, city, psychology		
ţ	butter, bottle		
tˀ	button		

IRREGULAR VERBS

base form	simple past	past participle	base form	simple past	past participle
be	was / were	been	leave	left	left
become	became	become	let	let	let
begin	began	begun	lose	lost	lost
break	broke	broken	make	made	made
bring	brought	brought	mean	meant	meant
build	built	built	meet	met	met
buy	bought	bought	pay	paid	paid
catch	caught	caught	put	put	put
choose	chose	chosen	quit	quit	quit
come	came	come	read /rid/	read /rɛd/	read /rɛd/
cost	cost	cost	ride	rode	ridden
cut	cut	cut	ring	rang	rung
do	did	done	rise	rose	risen
draw	drew	drawn	run	ran	run
dream	dreamed / dreamt	dreamed / dreamt	say	said	said
drink	drank	drunk	see	saw	seen
drive	drove	driven	sell	sold	sold
eat	ate	eaten	send	sent	sent
fall	fell	fallen	shake	shook	shaken
feed	fed	fed	sing	sang	sung
feel	felt	felt	sit	sat	sat
fight	fought	fought	sleep	slept	slept
find	found	found	speak	spoke	spoken
fit	fit	fit	spend	spent	spent
fly	flew	flown	stand	stood	stood
forget	forgot	forgotten	steal	stole	stolen
get	got	gotten	swim	swam	swum
give	gave	given	take	took	taken
go	went	gone	teach	taught	taught
grow	grew	grown	tell	told	told
have	had	had	think	thought	thought
hear	heard	heard	throw	threw	thrown
hit	hit	hit	understand	understood	understood
hold	held	held	wake up	woke up	woken up
hurt	hurt	hurt	wear	wore	worn
keep	kept	kept	win	won	won
know	knew	known	write	wrote	written

1 THE PRESENT OF <u>BE</u>

Statements

I	am	
You We They	are	late.
He She It	is	

2 THE SIMPLE PRESENT TENSE

Statements

I You We They	speak English.
He She	speaks English.

<u>Yes</u> / <u>no</u> questions

Do	I you we they	know them?
Does	he she	eat meat?

Short answers

Yes,	I you we they	do.
	he she it	does.

No,	I you we they	don't.
	he she it	doesn't.

Information questions

What do	you we they	need?
When does	he she it	start?
Who	wants needs likes	this book?

3 THE PRESENT CONTINUOUS

Statements

I	am	watching TV.
You We They	are	studying English.
He She It	is	arriving now.

<u>Yes</u> / <u>no</u> questions

Am	I	
Are	you we they	going too fast?
Is	he she it	

Short answers

Yes,	I	am.
	you	are.
	he she it	is.
	we they	are.

No,	I'm not.
	you aren't / you're not.
	he isn't / he's not.
	she isn't / she's not.
	it isn't / it's not.
	we aren't / we're not.
	they aren't / they're not.

Information questions

What	are	you we they	doing?
When	is	he she it	leaving?
Where	am	I	staying tonight?
Who	is		driving?

4 THE PAST OF <u>BE</u>

Statements

I He She It	was late.
We You They	were early.

(The past of be–continued)

Yes / no questions

Was	I he she it	on time?
Were	we you they	in the same class?

Short answers

Yes,	I he she it	was.
	we you they	were.

No,	I he she it	wasn't.
	we you they	weren't.

Information questions

Where	were	we? you? they?	
When	was	he she it	here?
Who	were	they?	
Who	was	he? she? it?	

5 THE SIMPLE PAST TENSE

Many verbs are irregular in the simple past tense.
See the list of irregular verbs on page 123.

Statements

I You He She It We They	stopped working.

I You He She It We They	didn't start again.

Yes / no questions

Did	I you he she it we they	make a good dinner?

Short answers

Yes,	I you he she it we they	did.

No,	I you he she it we they	didn't.

Information questions

When did	I you he she it we they	read that?
Who		called?

6 THE FUTURE WITH BE GOING TO

Statements

I'm You're He's She's It's We're They're	going to	be here soon.

I'm You're He's She's It's We're They're	not going to	be here soon.

Yes / no questions

Are	you we they	going to want coffee?
Am	I	going to be late?
Is	he she it	going to arrive on time?

Short answers

Yes,	I	am.
	you	are.
	he she it	is.
	we they	are.

No,	I'm not.
	you aren't / you're not.
	he isn't / he's not.
	she isn't / she's not.
	it isn't / it's not.
	we aren't / we're not.
	they aren't / they're not.

Information questions

What	are	you we they	going to see?
When	is	he she it	going to shop?
Where	am	I	going to stay tomorrow?
Who	is		going to call?

Grammar Booster

The Grammar Booster is optional. It offers a variety of information and extra practice. Sometimes it further explains or expands the unit grammar and points out common errors. In other cases, it reviews and practices previously learned grammar that would be helpful when learning new grammar concepts. If you use the Grammar Booster, you will find extra exercises in the Workbook in a separate section labeled Grammar Booster. The Grammar Booster content is not tested on any *Top Notch* tests.

UNIT 6 *Lesson 1*

Use to / used to: use and form

Use to and used to express a past habitual action, but one that is no longer true today.
> When I was a kid, I **didn't use to eat** vegetables. But now I do.

Remember: In yes / no questions and negative statements, use use to NOT used to.
> I **used** to stay up late. Now I don't.
> I **didn't use** to (NOT used to) get up early. Now I do.
> **Did** you **use** to (NOT used to) go dancing more often?

> **Note:** The simple past tense can express a past habitual action if there is a reference to a period of time in the past.
> > When I was a kid, I **didn't eat** peppers. I still don't today.

A On a separate sheet of paper, change each statement into a yes / no question.

> I used to go running every day. *Did you use to go running every day?*

1 There used to be a large tree in front of your house.

3 Their grandmother used to put sugar in their orange juice.

2 Mr. and Mrs. Palmer used to go dancing every weekend.

4 Luke used to be very overweight.

B On a separate sheet of paper, use the prompts to write logical sentences with negative or affirmative forms of use to / used to.

1 Jason and Trish / get lots of exercise, but now they go swimming every day.

2 There / be a movie theater on Smith Street, but now there isn't.

3 No one / worry about fatty foods, but now most people do.

4 English / be an international language, but now everyone uses English to communicate around the world.

5 Women in North America / wear pants, but now it's very common for them to wear them.

Be used to / get used to

Be used to + a noun phrase means to be accustomed to something. Compare use to / used to with be used to.
> I **didn't use to like** spicy food. But now I do. (used to + base form)
> I'm **used to the noise** now. But at first, it really bothered me. (be used to + a noun phrase)

Get used to + a noun phrase means to become accustomed to something.
> You'll **get used to the new menu** after a few days.

Be careful! With be used to, don't change used in negative statements or questions.
> He **wasn't used to** the weather there. NOT He wasn't ~~use to~~ . . .
> Are you **used to** life here? NOT Are you ~~use to~~ . . .

C   Check the sentences in which <u>used to</u> means "accustomed to something."

☐ 1 When the school term ended, I was finally used to the new teacher.
☐ 2 In our other class, the teacher used to be very strict.
☐ 3 They used to like red meat, but now they don't.
☐ 4 Because we lived in the mountains, we weren't used to fresh seafood.
☐ 5 I'm sure she'll get used to her new apartment soon.
☐ 6 These shoes used to be comfortable, but now they're too loose.
☐ 7 I'm sure she'll get used to wearing high-heeled shoes.

D   Write ✓ if the sentence is correct. Write ✗ if it is incorrect and make corrections.

☐ 1 I'll never get use to the traffic here.
☐ 2 We didn't use to take vacations very often.
☐ 3 Is he use to his new roommate yet?
☐ 4 Will she ever get use to life in the city?
☐ 5 What did you used to do on weekdays when you weren't working?

E   On a separate sheet of paper, write two sentences about something you're used to and two sentences about something you're not used to.

Repeated actions in the past: <u>would</u> + base form

You can also use <u>would</u> + the base form of a verb to describe repeated past actions. In this use, <u>would</u> has the same meaning as <u>used to</u>.

When we were young, our parents would go camping with us. (= used to go camping with us.)

Be careful! With non-action verbs that don't describe repeated actions, use <u>used to</u>, not <u>would</u>.
I used to have a lot of clothes. NOT I ~~would have~~ a lot of clothes.
My hometown used to be Dakar. NOT My hometown ~~would be~~ Dakar.
I used to be a terrible English student. NOT I ~~would be~~ a terrible English student.
My friends and I used to hate baseball. NOT My friends and I ~~would hate~~ baseball.

F   If it is possible, complete the sentence with <u>would</u>. If not, use a form of <u>used to</u>.

1 They .... go to the beach every Saturday in the summer.
2 I .... have a really large kitchen in my old house.
3 My husband never .... like coffee, but now he can't get enough of it.
4 Almost every evening of our vacation we .... eat at a terrific outdoor restaurant.
5 Before the microwave, people .... heat up soup on the top of the stove.
6 Sigrid .... be a tour guide, but now she's a professional chef.
7 There .... be three or four Italian restaurants in town, but now there aren't any.

UNIT 6 Lesson 2

Negative <u>yes</u> / <u>no</u> questions: short answers

Answer negative <u>yes</u> / <u>no</u> questions the same way as you would answer affirmative <u>yes</u> / <u>no</u> questions.

Is Jane a vegetarian?
Isn't Jane a vegetarian? | Yes, she is. / No, she isn't.

Do they have two sons?
Don't they have two sons? | Yes, they do. / No, they don't.

Answer each negative question with a short answer. (Use the information for your answer.)

1 A: Isn't Jeremy a lawyer?

B: .... He's not a lawyer.

2 A: Doesn't Bob have two brothers?

B: .... He has two younger brothers.

3 A: Haven't you been to Siberia before?

B: .... I've never been here before.

4 A: Aren't you learning English right now?

B: .... I'm studying English at the institute.

5 A: Wasn't Nancy at the movies last night?

B: .... She didn't go to the movies.

6 A: Don't Sachiko and Tomofumi have a car?

B: .... They own a minivan.

UNIT 7 *Lesson 1*

Gerunds and infinitives: usage within sentences

Gerunds (-ing form of a verb) and infinitives (to + base form) function as nouns within sentences.

Gerunds

Like nouns, gerunds can be subjects, subject complements, direct objects, and objects of prepositions.

Painting is my favorite leisure-time activity. (subject)

My favorite activity is painting. (subject complement; usually follows be)

I enjoy painting. (direct object)

I read a book about the history of painting. (object of the preposition of)

Infinitives

Infinitives can be subjects, subject complements, and direct objects.

To paint well is a talent. (subject)

The only thing he needs is to paint. (subject complement; usually follows be)

I want to paint. (direct object)

Underline the gerunds and circle the infinitives in these sentences. How is each used in the sentence? On the line next to each sentence, write *S* for subject, *C* for subject complement, *DO* for direct object, or *OP* for object of a preposition.

.... **1** I enjoy watching old movies every night on TV.

.... **2** Her greatest dream was to see all of her children attend college.

.... **3** What's the point of creating a nice environment at home if genetics is the only thing that counts?

.... **4** Avoiding too much pressure helps children become less critical.

.... **5** My niece plans to study personality development next semester.

UNIT 7 *Lesson 2*

Negative gerunds

A gerund can be made negative by using a negative word before it.

I like not going to bed too late.

They complained about never having enough time.

Complete the paragraph with affirmative and negative gerunds.

I really want to do something to improve my appearance and lose weight. I'm sick of .... able to fit into my
                                                                                          1 be
clothes. I know it's not enough to complain about .... weight—I need to do something about it! I plan to spend
                                                             2 gain
every afternoon .... my bike. Also, I want to go on a diet, but I'm afraid of .... hungry all the time.
                      3 ride   4 feel
I worry about .... enough energy to exercise if I'm .... enough to eat.
                    5 have   6 get

UNIT 8 Lesson 1

The passive voice: transitive verbs and intransitive verbs

A transitive verb can have a direct object. Transitive verbs can be used in the active voice or
passive voice.

active voice	passive voice

Picasso **painted** Guernica in 1937. → Guernica **was painted** in 1937.

An intransitive verb cannot have a direct object. With an intransitive verb, there is no "receiver"
of an action.
The painting **arrives** tomorrow.
The Mona Lisa **will stay** at the Louvre.
That new sculpture **looks** like a Botero.

Remember: The subject of a
sentence performs the action of
the verb. A direct object receives
the action of the verb.

Common intransitive verbs		
arrive	happen	sit
come	laugh	sleep
die	live	stand
fall	rain	stay
go	seem	walk

A Check each sentence that has an intransitive verb.

☐ 1 Pedro Almodóvar's new film arrives in theaters this fall.
☐ 2 A Canadian art collector has bought two of Michelangelo's drawings.
☐ 3 Someone stole Edvard Munch's painting The Scream in 2004.
☐ 4 The painter Georgia O'Keeffe lived in the southwestern part of the United States.
☐ 5 The Van Gogh Museum in Amsterdam sent Sunflowers on a world tour.
☐ 6 The traveling collection of ancient Roman sculpture is coming to San Diego this week.
☐ 7 The Metropolitan Museum of Art opened a new gallery last year.

The passive voice: form

Form the passive voice with a form of <u>be</u> and the past participle of a verb.

	Active voice	Passive voice
Simple present tense	Art collectors **buy** famous paintings all over the world.	Famous paintings **are bought** by art collectors all over the world.
Present continuous	The Film Center **is showing** Kurosawa's films.	Kurosawa's films **are being shown** at the Film Center.
Present perfect	Some world leaders **have bought** Yu Hung's paintings.	Yu Hung's paintings **have been bought** by some world leaders.
Simple past tense	I. M. Pei **designed** the Grand Pyramid at the Louvre.	The Grand Pyramid at the Louvre **was designed** by I. M. Pei.
Past continuous	In 2010, the museum **was selling** copies of Monet's paintings.	In 2010, copies of Monet's paintings **were being sold** by the museum.
Future with <u>will</u>	Ang Lee **will direct** a new film next year.	A new film **will be directed** by Ang Lee next year.
Future with <u>be going to</u>	The Tate Modern **is going to show** Van Gogh's drawings next month.	Van Gogh's drawings **are going to be shown** at the Tate Modern next month.

B   On a separate sheet of paper, rewrite each sentence in the passive voice. Use a <u>by</u> phrase only if it is important to know who is performing the action.

1   Someone actually stole the *Mona Lisa* in 1911.
2   Paloma Picasso designed these pieces of silver jewelry.
3   Someone will repair the sculpture when it gets old.
4   People have paid millions of U.S. dollars for some of Van Gogh's paintings.
5   They are showing some new paintings at the Smith Gallery this week.
6   The Malcolm Museum is going to exhibit ten sculptures by Asian artists.
7   Frida Kahlo was painting these pieces while she was sick in bed.
8   People built great pyramids throughout Central America during the height of the Mayan civilization.

C   On a separate sheet of paper, rewrite the sentences in Exercise A that have a transitive verb, changing the active voice to the passive voice.

UNIT 8   *Lesson 2*

The passive voice: <u>yes</u> / <u>no</u> questions

To form <u>yes</u> / <u>no</u> questions in the passive voice, move the first auxiliary verb before the subject.

Simple present tense	**Are** famous paintings <s>are</s> bought by art collectors?
Present continuous	**Are** Kurosawa's films <s>are</s> being shown at the Film Center?
Present perfect	**Have** Yu Hung's paintings <s>have</s> been bought by some world leaders?
Simple past tense	**Was** the Grand Pyramid at the Louvre <s>was</s> designed by I. M. Pei?
Past continuous	**Were** copies of Monet's paintings <s>were</s> being sold by the museum?
Future with <u>will</u>	**Will** a new film <s>will</s> be directed by Ang Lee next year?
Future with <u>be going to</u>	**Is** a collection of Van Gogh's drawings <s>is</s> going to be shown next month?

On a separate sheet of paper, rewrite the sentences as <u>yes</u> / <u>no</u> questions in the passive voice.

1   That new film about families is being directed by Gillian Armstrong.
2   One of da Vinci's most famous drawings has been sold by a German art collector.
3   A rare ceramic figure from the National Palace Museum in Taipei will be sent to the Metropolitan Museum of Art in New York.
4   A new exhibit is going to be opened at the Photography Gallery this week.
5   Some new paintings have been bought by the Prado Museum for their permanent collection.
6   *Las Meninas* can be seen at the Prado Museum in Madrid.
7   The *Jupiter* Symphony was written by Mozart.
8   Some of Michelangelo's work was being shown around the world in the 1960s.

Other ways to express a purpose

In order to

You can use <u>in order to</u> with a base form of a verb to express a purpose. The following three sentences have the same meaning.

I scrolled down in order to read the text.
I scrolled down because I wanted to read the text.
I scrolled down to read the text.

For

You can use <u>for</u> to express a purpose before a noun phrase or gerund phrase.

She e-mailed me for some advice.
They shop online for electronic products.
I use my smart phone for e-mailing clients.

Be careful! Don't use <u>for</u> before an infinitive of purpose.

DON'T SAY She e-mailed me for to ask a question.

A On a separate sheet of paper, rewrite the sentences with <u>in order to</u>.

1 She joined Facebook to meet new people.
2 Jason surfs the Internet to see what's new.
3 Alison uses online banking to pay all her bills.

4 They always print their documents first to read them carefully.
5 I never use the pull-down menu to open files.
6 He used an online telephone service to call his family.

B Complete each sentence with <u>for</u> or <u>to</u>.

1 My friend e-mailed me .... say he's getting married.
2 Jane shops online .... clothing.
3 I went online .... find a new keyboard.
4 Matt created a web page .... keeping in touch with his family and friends.

5 Sometimes I use my computer .... download movies.
6 We both log on to the Internet .... information.
7 Just click the icon .... open the file.
8 When Gina's computer crashed, her brother came over .... help her.

Comparison with adjectives: review

As . . . as

Use <u>as</u> . . . <u>as</u> to indicate how two things are equal or the same. Use <u>not as</u> . . . <u>as</u> to indicate how two things are different.

The new Jax 10 monitor is just as good as the Jax 20.
The Jax 10 monitor is not as big as the Jax 20.

Comparatives

Use comparatives to show how two things are not equal. Use <u>than</u> if the second item is mentioned.

My laptop is heavier than John's (is).   OR My laptop is heavier.
Regular mail is less convenient than e-mail. OR Regular mail is less convenient.

Superlatives

Use superlatives to show how one thing is different from two or more other things. Remember to use <u>the</u> with the superlative.

The M2, LX, and Bell printers are all good. But the Bell is the best.
The Gatt 40 monitor is the least expensive one you can buy.

A Correct the error in each sentence.

1 The Orca speakers aren't as heavier as the Yaltas.

2 My old laptop didn't have as many problems than my new laptop.

3 I checked out the three top brands, and the Piston was definitely the better.

4 Maxwell's web camera is much more expensive as their digital camera.

5 Of all the monitors I looked at, the X60 is definitely larger.

6 The Jaguar is most powerful computer in the world.

Comparison with adverbs

Comparatives
My new computer runs faster than my old one.
The X20 operates more quietly than the X30.

As . . . as
My new phone works as well as my old one.
The Macro laptop doesn't run as slowly as the Pell does.

Superlatives
Of these three laptops, the MPro starts up the most slowly.

Remember: Adverbs often give information about verbs.
My phone works **well**.   My printer prints **fast**.

Many adjectives can be changed to adverbs by adding -ly.

loud	→ **loudly**	quick	→ **quickly**	quiet	→ **quietly**
poor	→ **poorly**	bad	→ **badly**	slow	→ **slowly**

B On a separate sheet of paper, rewrite each pair of sentences into a single sentence using comparatives. Then write single sentences using as . . . as.

1 My brother's smart phone downloads music quickly. My MP3 player doesn't download quickly.

2 My new computer doesn't log on slowly. My old computer logs on slowly.

3 Your old monitor works well. My new monitor doesn't work well.

4 The Rico printer prints quickly. The Grant printer doesn't print quickly.

5 The Pace scanner doesn't run quietly. The Rico scanner runs quietly.

UNIT 10 *Lesson 1*

Should and ought to; had better

Use should or ought to + a base form to state an opinion or give advice, especially about an ethical choice. Ought to has the same meaning as should, but should is slightly less formal.
    You **should** (or **ought to**) return the wallet. You **shouldn't keep** it.

Use had better + a base form to state an opinion or give stronger advice. The meaning is similar to should and ought to, but had better expresses the idea that there is a consequence for not doing something.
    You'**d better tell** the waiter that the check is wrong. If you don't, he will have to pay.
    You'**d better not eat** at the Fairway Café. I got sick there the last time I did.

Remember: Should, ought to, and had better precede other verbs and give them a special meaning. They never change form.

Note: In American English it's very uncommon to use ought to in negative statements or questions. Use should or shouldn't instead.

A On a separate sheet of paper, complete the statements about an ethical choice, expressing your own ideas.

1 Colleagues in an office should always ....

2 Parents of young children should not ....

3 We ought to tell the store owner when ....

4 You forgot to pay your check? You had better ....

5 We had better not .... It's too expensive.

B On a separate sheet of paper, write five suggestions to a visitor to your country, using had better or had better not.

66 You'd better not take the local train to Bradbury. It's too slow. 77

Have to, must, and be supposed to

Have to and must

Use <u>have to</u> or the modal <u>must</u> + a base form to express obligation when there is no other choice of action available.

    Students **must take** this exam.

    You **have to take** the 6:00 train if you want to arrive on time.

Use <u>don't have to</u> (NOT <u>must</u>) to express a lack of obligation.

    You **don't have to pay** for the shoes if you don't like them. You can return them.

Use <u>must not</u> (NOT <u>don't have to</u>) for a strong or legal prohibition.

    Passengers **must not leave** their baggage unattended in the waiting area.

Be supposed to

Use <u>be supposed to</u> (or <u>not be supposed to</u>) + a base form to express an expected, but not a required, action. The degree of obligation is weaker than with <u>have to</u> or <u>must</u>.

    We're **supposed to pay** our check at the front of the coffee shop, not at the table. (The restaurant expects diners to pay at the front.)

    Hotel guests **are not supposed to use** the towels from their rooms at the pool.

> **Note:** <u>Must</u> is very formal and not very common in speaking. It is generally used by a person in authority (e.g., a teacher or boss) to state policy or law. <u>Have to</u> is much more common in both speaking and writing. The more informal <u>have got to</u> is also common in spoken English.
>
>   Sorry. I**'ve got to hurry**. I'm going to be late.
>
> Don't use <u>must not</u> for a lack of obligation. Use <u>don't have to</u> or <u>doesn't have to</u>.

C On a separate sheet of paper, write each sentence two ways: with <u>must</u> and with <u>have to</u>.

  1 Drivers / obey the speed limit.

  2 Students / arrive on time for class.

  3 In this beach restaurant / diners / wear shoes. If you are barefoot, don't come in.

  4 You / have a reservation to eat at the Palace Restaurant.

D On a separate sheet of paper, write five sentences that describe actions your school expects from its students. Use <u>be supposed to</u>.

> *Students are supposed to come on time to class. They're not supposed to be late.*

E Choose the sentence closer in meaning to each numbered statement or question.

  1 Do you think the Milton Restaurant is a good place to eat?

    a Do you think I should eat at the Milton Restaurant?

    b Do you think I have to eat at the Milton Restaurant?

  2 If you don't have a reservation, the restaurant won't give you a table.

    a The restaurant is supposed to give you a table.

    b You had better have a reservation.

  3 They don't accept credit cards in this store. They only accept cash.

    a You have to pay with cash.

    b You ought to pay with cash.

  4 Don't wear shorts in the restaurant.

    a You must not wear shorts in the restaurant.

    b You don't have to wear shorts in the restaurant.

UNIT 10 Lesson 2

Possessive nouns: review and expansion

Add <u>'s</u> (an apostrophe + <u>s</u>) to a name or a singular noun.

    Where is Glenn's car?   What's your daughter's married name?

    This is Ms. Baker's class.   I love Dickens's novels.

Add an apostrophe to plural nouns that end in <u>s</u>. For irregular plurals, such as <u>women</u> or <u>children</u>, add <u>'s</u>.

    the women's room   the boys' clothes   the Jacksons' car

Add <u>'s</u> to the name or noun that comes last in a list of two or more.

    Jean and Ralph's house

A Correct the following sentences, adding an apostrophe or an apostrophe + s to the possessive nouns.

Carmen's jacket is under the table.

1 The two girls keys are lost.
2 Mr. Stiller English is really fluent.
3 The doctor office is downstairs.
4 Sarah and Tom children are at the Taylor School.

5 That man car is parked in a no-parking zone.
6 Julia friend brother is going to get married tonight.
7 The Smiths garden is beautiful.

Pronouns: summary

Subject pronouns

Subject pronouns represent subject nouns and noun phrases. The subject pronouns are I, you, he, she, it, we, and they.

Matt didn't break the plate = He didn't break the plate.

Object pronouns

Object pronouns represent nouns (and noun phrases) that function as direct objects, indirect objects, and objects of prepositions. The object pronouns are me, you, him, her, it, us, and them.

They gave Susan the toy car for the children.
They gave it to her for them.

B On a separate sheet of paper, rewrite the sentences, replacing the underlined nouns and noun phrases with pronouns.

Matt didn't break the plate. *He didn't break it.*

1 Our children love TV.
2 Janet and I never buy food at that store.
3 Do you and I have the car this afternoon?
4 Sylvia's family laughs at her jokes.
5 My friends are speaking with Ms. Rowe today.

6 Mr. Harris is teaching the students with Mr. Cooper.
7 All the students are speaking English very well this year.
8 Does Carl need to give the paper to his teachers?
9 Martin and Larry returned the money to the woman.

Writing Booster

The Writing Booster is optional. It is intended to teach students the conventions of written English. Each unit's Writing Booster is focused both on a skill and its application to the Writing exercise from the Unit Review page.

UNIT 6 Connecting ideas: subordinating conjunctions

A subordinating conjunction connects a dependent clause to an independent clause.

Subordinating conjunctions	
because	unless
since	although
if	(even) though

——— independent clause ———   ——— dependent clause ———
People are eating more fast foods today **because** they want to save time.
I generally avoid carbohydrates **even though** it isn't easy.

A dependent clause can also come at the beginning of a sentence. Use a comma after the dependent clause when it comes first.

——— dependent clause ———   ——— independent clause ———
Because people want to save time, they are eating more fast foods today.
Even though it isn't easy, I generally avoid carbohydrates.

Use the subordinating conjunction <u>if</u> to express a condition. Use <u>unless</u> to express a negative condition.
You will be healthy **if** you eat right and exercise regularly.
You will gain weight **unless** you eat right and exercise regularly. (= if you don't)

Use the subordinating conjunctions <u>although</u>, <u>even though</u>, or <u>though</u> to express a contradiction.
Although
Even though   they knew fatty foods were unhealthy, people ate them anyway.
Though

Remember: Use <u>because</u> or <u>since</u> to give a reason.

A Choose the best subordinating conjunction to complete each sentence.

1 (Though / If / Unless) I learn to speak English well, I will be very happy.

2 (Even though / Because / If) she is an artist, she is interested in science.

3 Studying English is important (although / because / unless) it can help you do more.

4 (Unless / Although / Since) English grammar isn't easy, I like studying it.

5 They have to go on a diet (because / unless / though) they're overweight.

6 He cut back on desserts and sodas (even though / if / because) he didn't want to.

7 (Even though / Because / Unless) my grandmother is 80 years old, she is in very good health.

8 (Unless / Because / Though) I think I'm going to get sick, I don't want to change my eating habits.

9 She won't eat red meat (because / unless / although) she has to.

10 (Unless / Even though / Since) she's a vegetarian, she sometimes eats fish.

B Read each sentence. Then, on a separate sheet of paper, write and connect a clause to the sentence, using the subordinating conjunction.

1 Most people don't want to change their eating habits. (even though)

2 Children become overweight. (if)

3 Obesity will continue to be a global problem. (unless)

4 Eating too much fast food is bad for you. (because)

5 Most people continue to eat unhealthy foods. (although)

> *1 Most people don't want to change their eating*
> *habits even though they have health problems.*

C Guidance for the Writing Exercise (on page 72) Using four different subordinating conjunctions, write four sentences: two about eating habits in the past and two about eating habits in the present. Use your sentences in your paragraph about eating habits.

UNIT 7 Parallel structure

When writing a series of words or phrases in a sentence, be sure that all items in the series are in the same grammatical form. This feature of good writing is called "parallel structure."

Lucy is creative. She likes painting, playing the piano, and dancing. (all items in the series are gerunds)

Be careful! Don't combine gerunds and infinitives in the same series.
Don't write: Lucy is creative. She likes painting, ~~to play~~ the piano, and dancing.

In a series of infinitives, it is correct to use to before each item in the series or to use to only before the first item.

✗ I decided to study medicine, get married, and ~~to~~ have children before my thirtieth birthday.

✓ I decided to study medicine, to get married, and to have children before my thirtieth birthday.

✓ I decided to study medicine, get married, and have children before my thirtieth birthday.

Remember: When a sentence includes a series of more than two words or phrases, separate them with commas. Use and before the last item in the series. The comma before and is optional.

no comma (two items)   commas (three items)

Jake and May have three favorite activities: painting, singing, and dancing.

A Correct the errors in parallel structure in the sentences.

1 I have begun studying psychology and to learn about personality development.

2 They avoid arguing about the nature-nurture controversy and to disagree about which is more important.

3 The Bersons love to run, to swim, and lift weights.

4 She's both responsible and social. She prefers to study early in the evening and going out afterwards.

5 Introverts hate to talk about their feelings and being with a lot of people.

6 Marjorie is a classic extrovert. She likes to be very active, knowing a lot of people, and to seek excitement.

7 To be quiet, be hard to know, and to seek peace are traits typical of the introvert's personality.

8 Psychologists of the nineteenth century continued believing in the importance of genetics and to write about it in books and articles.

B Guidance for the Writing Exercise (on page 84) On a separate sheet of paper, write sentences to answer some or all the following questions about the person you chose. If appropriate, use verbs and phrases from the box on the right. Be careful to use parallel structure. Use the sentences in your paragraphs about the person.

- Who is the person?
- What is his or her relation to you?
- Who are the people in his or her family?
- How many siblings does he or she have?
- What kind of personality does he or she have?
- What are his or her likes and dislikes?
- Are there some things he or she is excited about, bored with, angry about, or worried about right now?
- Are there some things he or she is excited about, bored with, angry about, or worried about right now?

Words to describe likes / dislikes	
avoids	hopes
hates	would like
can't stand	is happy about
doesn't mind	is excited about
enjoys	is bored with
expects	is sick and tired of

Remember: A good paragraph has a topic sentence that clearly states what the main idea of the paragraph is.

In addition, a paragraph should have **supporting details**—that is, information that provides support for, and is clearly tied to, the topic sentence.

Be careful! If a detail doesn't support the topic sentence or isn't tied to it clearly, then it may not belong in the paragraph.

In the writing model to the right, the topic sentence of the paragraph is highlighted in yellow. The sentences that follow are details. Two of the sentences are crossed out because they do not support the topic sentence and should not be included in the paragraph. These two sentences do not provide information about the chair and do not indicate why the writer likes the chair. The remaining sentences are supporting details—they all support the topic sentence and are clearly tied to it. They provide more information about the chair and they explain why the writer likes the chair.

> In my living room, my favorite possession is an old wooden chair. My parents gave it to me when I left home. A wooden chair can be very expensive if it is an antique. It has lots of memories for me because it was in my parents' bedroom when I was growing up. It's important to take very good care of wooden furniture. The chair is very comfortable, and I used to sit in it a lot as a child.

A Read each topic sentence. Circle the detail that does not support the topic sentence.

1 Many French artists in the nineteenth century were influenced by Japanese art and printmaking.
   a Today, the work of Hokusai, Japan's most famous printmaker, is popular in Western countries.
   b Looking at the work of the French impressionists, it is clear that they chose to imitate the Japanese artistic styles of the time.
   c A number of French artists had collections of Japanese art.

2 I love my poster of Álvaro Saborío, the Costa Rican soccer player, but my wife hates it.
   a I think Saborío is a great player.
   b My wife doesn't think I should keep it in our bedroom.
   c The number on Saborío's uniform is 15.

3 Rodin's statue, *The Thinker*, is probably one of the most famous sculptures in the world.
   a This metal sculpture of a man deep in thought is recognized all over the world.
   b Rodin was born on November 12, 1840.
   c The image of *The Thinker* can be seen in popular art and advertisements.

4 On a side table in my dining room, I have two small ceramic figures of lions from my trip to Taipei.
   a They have beautiful colors including red, green, blue, and yellow.
   b You should visit the National Palace Museum when you are in Taipei.
   c I bought them together from a small shop at a temple I was visiting.

5 My sister has always shown a lot of talent in the performing arts.
   a We've had our differences, and we haven't always agreed on everything.
   b She has acted in school plays since she was about ten years old.
   c I think she's going to follow a career as an actor or dancer.

6 I think artistic talent is something you're born with.
   a I've tried many times to improve my ability at drawing, but it hasn't worked.
   b I have friends who are very talented in art, but they've never taken any special classes.
   c My aunt studied art at the Art Institute of Chicago for four years.

B   **Guidance for the Writing Exercise (on page 96)** On the notepad, write the favorite object you chose. Create a topic sentence that states the most important thing you want to say about that object. Then write five supporting details to use in your paragraph.

Favorite object:

Topic sentence:

Details to support my topic sentence:

1.

2.

3.

4.

5.

UNIT **9**   Organizing ideas

When you want to describe the benefits and problems of an issue, there are different ways you can organize your ideas. Here are some approaches.

Approach 1: In one paragraph
One way is to describe all the advantages and disadvantages in one paragraph. Following are notes of the details that will be included in the paragraph.

> THE ADVANTAGES AND DISADVANTAGES OF SMART PHONES
>
> Advantages: are easy to carry, don't miss calls, keep you connected with family and friends
>
> Disadvantages: bother other people, make people dependent, are easy to lose

This approach is good for a short piece of writing consisting of only a few sentences. However, if you want to develop those ideas in more than just a few sentences, it is easier for the reader to follow if you can organize the details in one of the following ways:

Approach 2: In two paragraphs
In this approach, you can use a first paragraph to describe all the advantages. Then you can use a second paragraph to describe all the disadvantages. Following are notes of the details that will be included in each paragraph.

> Paragraph 1: SMART PHONES HAVE ADVANTAGES
>
> are easy to carry, don't miss calls, keep you connected with family and friends
>
> Paragraph 2: BUT THEY ALSO HAVE DISADVANTAGES
>
> bother other people, make people dependent, are easy to lose

Approach 3: In more than two paragraphs
In this approach, you can use a separate paragraph to focus on each different topic. In each paragraph, you can describe both advantages and disadvantages. Following are notes of the details that will be included in each paragraph.

> Paragraph 1: (THEY'RE SMALL.) smart phones easy to carry, but also easy to lose
>
> Paragraph 2: (THEY'RE CONVENIENT.) won't miss calls, but you can also bother other people
>
> Paragraph 3: (THEY'VE CHANGED OUR LIVES.) keep people connected with family and friends, but also
>
> can make people dependent

A   Using Approach 2, organize the ideas into two paragraphs: paragraph 1 is about the benefits of renting a car; paragraph 2 is about the problems. Write 1 or 2 next to each idea.

____ It gives you the freedom to go wherever you want to go whenever you want.

____ You might see places you can't see by bus or train.

____ You could have an accident during your trip.

____ You have more control over whether or not you will have an accident during your trip.

____ You can carry more luggage and other things you might need.

____ To drive safely, you have to become familiar with the local driving rules.

____ If you're traveling with a group of people, it could cost less than paying for bus and train tickets.

____ You may have to understand road signs that are in a different language.

____ If you have to do all the driving, it can be very stressful and tiring.

____ If you're traveling alone or with one other person, it could cost a lot of money in rental fees and gas.

B   Now, on a separate sheet of paper, practice using Approach 3. Organize the sentences from Exercise A by topic into three or more separate paragraphs. Don't forget to include a topic sentence.

C   Guidance for the Writing Exercise (on page 108) Use your notes on page 107 to write your paragraphs about the benefits and problems of the Internet. Choose Approach 2 or Approach 3 to organize your writing.

UNIT 10   Introducing conflicting ideas: On the one hand; On the other hand

Use On the one hand and On the other hand to present conflicting ideas or two sides of an issue. The following two sentences present the two sides together, one right after the other.

On the one hand, I would want to tell the truth. On the other hand, I wouldn't want to get in trouble.

Remember: You can also present conflicting or contradictory information with Even though, Although, and However.

Even though I'm basically an honest person, I don't always tell the truth.
Although Matt didn't think he broke the dish, it's possible that he did.
Matt wanted to tell the owner of the store what happened. However, Noah didn't agree.

When one paragraph presents one side of an issue and the next one presents the other, writers don't usually use On the one hand in the first paragraph. Instead, they just begin the next paragraph with On the other hand to let the reader know that the conflicting idea will follow. Look at the writing model to the right.

Being honest has many advantages. If you always tell the truth, you don't have to remember an untruth you said before. People who tell the truth don't have trouble sleeping. They can look at themselves in the mirror and feel good.

On the other hand, there are times when telling a lie makes sense. For example, your friend Andrew might ask you if you like his new jacket, and you think it's ugly. If you told him that, it would hurt his feelings. It's possible that not being absolutely truthful might make more sense.

A   Reread the Photo Story on page 111. Write a summary of the story in three to five sentences. Answer the questions below.

• Where was Matt?   • What happened?

• Who was he with?   • What did the two friends discuss?

B   Answer the questions below. Write three to five sentences about Matt's choices. Then write the consequences of each choice. Use If and the unreal conditional in at least one sentence.

• What should he do?   • What could he do?   • What would most people do?

C   Write three to five sentences about what you would do if you were Matt. Answer the questions below.

• What would you do?   • What would happen if you did that?   • What would happen if you didn't?

D   Guidance for the Writing Exercise (on page 120) In your paragraphs about Matt's dilemma, use On the one hand, On the other hand, Even though, Although, and However to connect conflicting ideas.

Top Notch Pop Lyrics

▶ 1:16–1:17 **Greetings and Small Talk**
[Unit 1]
You look so familiar. Have we met before?
I don't think you're from around here.
It might have been two weeks ago, but I'm
not sure.
Has it been a month or a year?
I have a funny feeling that I've met you twice.
That's what they call déjà vu.
You were saying something friendly, trying to
be nice—and now you're being friendly, too.
One look, one word.
It's the friendliest sound that I've ever heard.
Thanks for your greetings.
I'm glad this meeting occurred.

(CHORUS)
Greetings and small talk
make the world go round.
On every winding road I've walked,
this is what I've found.

Have you written any letters to your friends
back home?
Have you had a chance to do that?
Have you spoken to your family on the
telephone?
Have you taken time for a chat?
Bow down, shake hands.
Do whatever you do in your native land.
I'll be happy to greet you
in any way that you understand.

(CHORUS)

Have you seen the latest movie out of
Hollywood?
Have you read about it yet?
If you haven't eaten dinner, are you in the
mood for a meal you won't forget?
Bow down, shake hands.
Do whatever you do in your native land.
I'll be happy to greet you
in any way that you understand.

(CHORUS)

▶ 1:35–1:36 **Better Late Than Never**
[Unit 2]
Where have you been? I've waited for you.
I'd rather not say how long.
The movie began one hour ago.
How did you get the time all wrong?
Well, I got stuck in traffic, and when I arrived
I couldn't find a parking place.
Did you buy the tickets? You're kidding—
for real?
Let me pay you back, in that case.

(CHORUS)
Sorry I'm late.
I know you've waited here forever.
How long has it been?
It's always better late than never.

When that kind of movie comes to the
big screen,
it always attracts a crowd,
and I've always wanted to see it with you—
but it looks like we've missed it now.
I know what you're saying, but actually,
I would rather watch a video.

So why don't we rent it and bring it
back home?
Let's get in the car and go.

(CHORUS)

Didn't you mention, when we made our
plans, that you've seen this movie recently?
It sounds so dramatic, and I'm so upset,
I'd rather see a comedy!
Well, which comedy do you recommend?
It really doesn't matter to me.
I still haven't seen 'The World and a Day'.
I've heard that one is pretty funny.

(CHORUS)

▶ 2:17–2:18 **Checking Out** [Unit 3]
Ms. Jones travels all alone.
She doesn't need much space—
a single room with a nice twin bed
and a place for her suitcase.
Her stay is always satisfactory,
but in the morning she's going to be
checking out.
Mr. Moon will be leaving soon,
and when he does I'll say,
"Thank you, sir, for staying with us.
How do you want to pay?"
And in the end it isn't hard.
He'll put it on his credit card. He's
checking out.
Would you like to leave a message?
Could you call back later?
Do you need some extra towels
or today's newspaper?
Can I get you anything?
Would you like room service?
I'm so sorry.
Am I making you nervous?
Good evening.
I'll ring that room for you.
Is that all?
I'll be glad to put you through.
I'm sorry, but he's not answering.
The phone just rings and rings.
The couple in room 586
have made a king-size mess.
Pick up the laundry. Turn down the beds.
We have another guest
coming with his family.
You'd better hurry or they will be
checking out. . .

▶ 2:36–2:37 **Wheels around the
World** [Unit 4]
Was I going too fast
or a little too slow?
I was looking out the window,
and I just don't know.
I must have turned the steering wheel
a little too far
when I drove into the bumper
of that luxury car.
Oh no!
How awful!
What a terrible day!
I'm sorry to hear that.
Are you OK?

(CHORUS)
Wheels around the World
are waiting here with your car.
Pick it up.
Turn it on.
Play the radio.
Wheels around the World—
"helping you to go far."
You can drive anywhere.
Buckle up and go.

Did I hit the red sedan,
or did it hit me?
I was talking on the cell phone
in my SUV.
Nothing was broken,
and no one was hurt,
but I did spill some coffee
on my favorite shirt.
Oh no!
Thank goodness you're still alive!
I'm so happy that
you survived.

(CHORUS)

What were you doing when you hit that tree?
I was racing down the mountain, and the
brakes failed me.
How did it happen? Was the road still wet?
Well, there might have been a danger sign,
But I forget.
The hood popped open and the door fell off.
The headlights blinked and the
engine coughed.
The side-view mirror had a terrible crack.
The gearshift broke. Can I bring the
car back?
Oh no!
Thank goodness
you're still alive!
I'm so happy that
you survived.

(CHORUS)

▶ 3:17–3:18 **Piece of Cake** [Unit 5]
I need to pick up a few things
on the way back to school.
Feel like stopping at a store with me?
I'd like to, but I think I'll pass.
I don't have time today.
It's already nearly a quarter to three.

(CHORUS)
Don't worry. We'll be fine.
How long can it take?
It's easy. It'll be a piece of cake.

I need a tube of toothpaste and
a bar of Luvly soap,
some sunscreen, and a bottle of shampoo.
Where would I find makeup?
How about a comb?
Have a look in aisle one or two.

(CHORUS)

I have an appointment
for a haircut at The Spa.
On second thought, they're always
running late.
My class starts in an hour.
I'll never make it now.
How long do you think we'll have to wait?

(CHORUS)

They say there's someone waiting
for a trim ahead of me.
Can I get you some coffee or some tea?
OK. In the meantime,
I'll be getting something strong
for this headache at the pharmacy!

(CHORUS)

▶ 3:37–3:38 **A Perfect Dish** [Unit 6]

I used to eat a lot of fatty foods,
but now I just avoid them.
I used to like chocolate and lots of sweets,
but now those days are gone.
To tell you the truth,
it was too much trouble.
They say you only live once,
but I'm not crazy about feeling sick.
What was going wrong?
Now I know I couldn't live without this.
Everything's ready.
Why don't you sit down?

(CHORUS)
**It looks terrific,
but it smells pretty awful.
What in the world can it be?
It smells like chicken,
and it tastes like fish—
a terrific dish
for you and me—
a perfect dish for you
and me.**

I used to be a big meat eater,
now I'm vegetarian,
and I'm not much of a coffee drinker.
I can't stand it anymore.
I'm avoiding desserts with sugar.
I'm trying to lose some weight.
Some things just don't agree with me.
They're bad for me, I'm sure.
Would you like some?
Help yourself.
Isn't it so good for you health?

(CHORUS)

Aren't you going to have some?
Don't you like it?
Wasn't it delicious?
Don't you want some more?

(CHORUS)

▶ 4:13–4:14 **The Colors of Love** [Unit 7]

Are you sick and tired of working hard day
and night?
Do you like to look at the world in shades of
black and white?
Your life can still be everything that you were
dreaming of.
Just take a look around you and see all the
colors of love.
You wake up every morning and go through
the same old grind.
You don't know how the light at the window
could be so unkind. If blue is the color that
you choose when the road is rough, you know
you really need to believe in the colors of love.

(CHORUS)
**The colors of love
are as beautiful as a rainbow.**

The colors of love
shine on everyone in the world.
Are negative thoughts and emotions painful
to express?
They're just tiny drops in the ocean of
happiness.
And these are the feelings you must learn to
rise above.
Your whole life is a picture you paint with the
colors of love.

(CHORUS)

▶ 4:28–4:29 **To Each His Own** [Unit 8]

He doesn't care for Dali.
The colors are too bright.
He says that Picasso
got everything just right.
She can't stand the movies
that are filmed in Hollywood.
She likes Almodóvar.
She thinks he's really good.
He's inspired by everything
she thinks is second-rate.
She's moved and fascinated
by the things he loves to hate.
He's crazy about art that only
turns her heart to stone.
I guess that's why they say
to each his own.
He likes pencil drawings.
She prefers photographs.
He takes her to the the art museum,
but she just laughs and laughs.
He loves the Da Vinci
that's hanging by the door.
She prefers the modern art
that's lying on the floor.
"No kidding! You'll love it. Just wait and see.
It's perfect in every way."
She shakes her head. "It's not for me.
It's much too old and gray."
She thinks he has the worst taste
that the world has ever known.
I guess that's why they say
to each his own.
But when it's time to say goodbye,
they both feel so alone.
I guess that's why they say
to each his own.

▶ 5:16–5:17 **Life in Cyberspace** [Unit 9]

I'm just fooling around.
Am I interrupting you?
Well, I wanted to know—
what are you up to?
I tried to send some photos,
but it's been so long
that I almost don't remember
how to log on.
So I'm thinking about getting a
new computer.
I don't know what kind. I should have done
it sooner.
But I heard the Panatel is as good as
the rest.
Check it out. Check it out.
You should really check it out.

(CHORUS)
**Let's face it—that's life.
That's life in cyberspace.**

When you download the pictures,
then you open the files.
If your computer's slow,
then it can take a little while.
From the pull-down menu,
you can print them, too.
But don't forget to save
everything you do.
Scroll it up. Scroll it down.
Put your cursor on the bar.
Then click on the icon,
and you'll see my new car!
The car goes as fast
as the one I had before.
Check it out. Check it out.
You should really check it out.

(CHORUS)

Am I talking to myself, or are you still there?
This instant message conversation's
going nowhere.
I could talk to Liz.
She isn't nearly as nice.
It isn't quite as much fun.
I've done it once or twice.
What's the problem?
Come on. Give it a try.
If you don't want to be friends,
at least tell me why.
Did you leave to make a call
or go out to get some cash?
Did the photos I sent make your
computer crash?

(CHORUS)

▶ 5:31–5:32 **What Would You Do?**
[Unit 10]

What would you do
if I got a tattoo with your name?
What would you say
if I dyed my hair for you?
What would you do
if I sang outside your window?
What would you think
if I told you I loved you?

(CHORUS)
**I hate to say this,
but I think you're making a big mistake.
By tomorrow,
I'm sure you'll be sorry.**

What would you do
if I sent you a love letter?
Would you say it was wrong
and send it back to me?
What would you think
if I pierced my ears? Would you care?
Would you think
that I had lost all my modesty?

(CHORUS)

Well, give it some thought.
I know I could make you happy.
Are you kidding?
You'd have to be nuts to ask me.
It's no mistake. I'm sure
that my heart is yours.
I have to find a way
to make you mine.

(CHORUS)